The Arch
of
Mag

The Archidoxes

of

Magic

by
Paracelsus

Of the Supreme Mysteries of Nature
Of the Spirits of the Planets
Of the Secrets of Alchymy
Of Occult Philosophy
The Mysteries of the twelve Signs of the Zodiack
The Magical Cure of Diseases

Of Celestial Medicines

Translation by Robert Turner

Introduction by Stephen Skinner

Ibis Press
An Imprint of Nicolas-Hays, Inc.
Berwick, Maine

First English edition 1656
Second English edition 1975
This edition published 2004 by Ibis Press,
an imprint of Nicolas-Hays, Inc.,
P. O. Box 1126, Berwick, ME 03901-1126
www.nicolashays.com

Distributed to the trade by Red Wheel/Weiser LLC,
P. O. Box 612, York Beach, ME 03910-0612
www.redwheelweiser.com

Library of Congress Cataloging-in-Publication Data available on request.

ISBN 0-89254-097-4

Cover design by Daniel Brockman

MV
Printed in the United States of America

10	09	08	07	06	05	04
7	6	5	4	3	2	1

The paper used in this publication meets the minimum requirements of the American National Standard for Information Sciences—Permanence of Paper for Printed Library Materials Z39.48–1992 (R1997).

INTRODUCTION

The life of Paracelsus, or to give him his full name, Philippus Aureolus
Theophrastus Bombastus von Hohenheim (1493–1541) reads like a
romance, grown and elaborated from the whole canon of alchemical
legend and history. His vast learning and quest-like travelling, the
constant merging of truth and speculation, makes his character the
most interesting in the whole history of magical and alchemical research.

He was born in Einsiedeln near Zurich in 1493 amidst the beginnings
of the intellectual turmoil of the Renaissance, a time in which his
iconoclastic genius must have felt at home, despite the years of persecu-
tion he suffered for his revolutionary ideas.

He was the son of a physician and his early education was gained in
the mining school founded by the Fuggers of Ausburg. He attended
Basel University and visited the Universities of Vienna, Cologne and
Paris. His knowledge of the magical tradition derived however from
the time he spent with Johannes Trithemius, Abbot of Sponheim and
later of Würzburg. Trithemius was also the teacher of Cornelius
Agrippa in matters magical, and indirectly responsible for the latter's
De Occulta Philosophia.

At twenty-three Paracelsus began his travels which took him from
Spain to Moscow, Constantinople to Sweden. He studied the Moorish
Galenic system of medicine in Montpellier, visited mines in Cornwall
and Cumberland, and served as an army surgeon in Venice and the
Netherlands. In Russia he was taken prisoner by the Tartars, only to
rise to a position of prominence in their court, eventually being sent
as a companion to the Prince's son on a journey to Constantinople. At
this point myth clouds the truth and there is talk of his being given the
secret of Transmutation or the Elixir, by an Arabian. According to
Von Helmont's *History of the Tartars*, Paracelsus came to Constantinople
during 1521 and received the Philosopher's Stone from Solomon
Trismosin, the author of one of the most exquisitely executed works
on the twenty-two stages of alchemy—*Splendor Solis.*

In 1526 Paracelsus bought a citizenship of Strassburg and prepared .
to settle down. He was soon appointed a practising physician, having
added Erasmus to his long list of patients, and before the year was out
he was offered the position of city physician and the professorship of
medicine as Basel.

In the university he was viewed with suspicion when he tried to
propagate his ideas on the reform of medical theory and practice,

especially as he was the first man to teach in the German language in a German University, Latin being the language of the scholars of his day.

During the Feast of St. John, Paracelsus arrived at the University holding in his hand Avicenna's canon of medicine which he unceremoniously flung into the flames: it was his challenge to the old school. He then led his students into the surrounding country to study herbal medicines 'where God has placed them'. His lectures, his treatment and his character were defamed. He was 'the Luther of medicine', 'a vagabond who assumed the title of doctor', 'necromancer' and an 'ox-head'. He was not slow to retaliate: the doctors were 'a misbegotten crew of approved asses', the apothecaries 'scullions' and their potions 'foul broths'.

His aggressive manner (and famous cures) soon earned him enough enemies for him to begin again the circuitous secretive wanderings that characterised so much of his life.

During his wanderings Paracelsus developed the doctrine of Signatures which he had inherited from Albertus Magnus, and which was reinforced by his own acute observation and use of herbal remedies. The theory is based on the idea that every part of man, the microcosmic world, corresponds to some part of the universe, the macrocosmic world, and that the connection will be obvious by some similarity of form or colour, in fact by its Signature. For example, certain leaves have tracings on them which appear not unlike the outline of certain organs of the body: these then, according to the doctrine, are suitable for treating diseases of that organ.

Associated with his doctrine of Signatures are his ideas on Specifics. He realised that the maze of incredible cures and mixtures often prescribed in the writings of Galenists was ridiculously complicated, contrary to common sense and mostly ineffective. Paracelsus decided that mineral, plant and animal substances contained what he called 'active principles'. Accordingly he searched for a method whereby these substances could be purified and intensified to release these 'active principles' which would then be more efficacious and much safer to administer than in their crude and often dangerous original form.

The publication in 1536 of Paracelsus' *Greater Surgery* restored to him the fame depreciated by academic and sacedotal cabals. It contrasted severely with the medical theory of his period which was based on the accepted doctrines of Hippocrates, Avicenna and Galen. Amongst his fellow physicians, no experiments were encouraged, and no doctrines or opinions tolerated that might be in evident contradiction with these sacred authorities. The doctrines of medical science were a closed book just as the authority of the church was final. They might be commented on, expounded, interpreted and taught, but not contradicted nor seriously questioned. Paracelsus' medical theory on the other hand was closely related to natural philosophy, experience and observation.

Paracelsus' system was based on Neoplatonic Philosophy in which the life of man is regarded as inseparable from that of the universe.

For him, the scriptual *limus terrae* from which the body of man is created is in reality an extract of all beings previously created. It is primarily a compound of 'salt', 'sulphur' and 'mercury'; the separation of these elements in man being the cause of sickness. This separation is due to the failure of the *archaeus* (the vital force situated in the stomach) in performing its function of separating the useful from the poisonous.

For the treatment of disease Paracelsus discovered opium, introduced mineral baths, mercury, lead, sulphur, arsenic and copper sulphate, a large part of the then known pharmacopoeia, and popularised tinctures and alcoholic extracts. To what extent these new methods were original to him and to what extent accumulated during his wanderings in foreign lands, it is not possible to determine.

On a more subtle level the unique achievement of Paracelsus was to accentuate the link between chemical experiment and spiritual enlightenment. It has become quite clear that alchemy must deal simultaneously with the alchemist himself, both spiritually and physically.

Paracelsus died on September 24, 1541, in Salzburg, allegedly the victim of a drunken brawl. His more discreet biographers have always cast doubt upon this end, but it is not at all inconsistent with his character. His body is buried in St. Sebastian's Church, but Paracelsus' memory has blossomed in the dust to sainthood, for the poor have canonised him and still pray there.

It is difficult to ascertain with any degree of certainty which writings are genuinely by Paracelsus and which are spurious, as most of his writings were dictated to his pupils, and few of his works were actually printed during his lifetime. After his death, his disciples were apparently very careless in their preparation of his manuscripts for the printers, and many errors have crept into the printed versions of his writings.

Of the numerous editions of his works brought out by Fridericus Bitiskius in 1658, Forberger and Bodenstein in 1575, Hieronymus Feierabend in Frankfurt, Arnold Byrkmann in Cologne, Peter Barna in Basel and by John Huser (Strassburg 1603 and Cologne 1589) only the latter is fairly reliable. Even so it certainly includes works written by some of Paracelsus' disciples such as Adam von Bodenstein, Alexander von Suchten, Gerhard Dorn, Leonhard Thurneyssen, Peter Severinus, Oswald Croll and Melchoir Schennemann, as well as works probably falsely attributed to Paracelsus. The Huser edition of Paracelsus contains the *Archidoxes Magicae* which is one of the most practical of works on magic written by Paracelsus.

The present translation was made by Robert Turner in 1655. Turner was also responsible for other translations of works by Paracelsus, the *Ars Notoria*, Cornelius Agrippa's *De Occulta Philosophia* and several other extremely important works on practical magic. All of these works profoundly affected Dr. John Dee and later Francis Barrett, both key figures in occultism in England. John Dee's experiments with angel magic and scrying between 1581 and 1608 relied to a large extent on

Agrippa's work, whilst Barrett used Turner's translation to compile *The Magus* in 1801, the last synthetic work covering the whole field of qabalistic magic till the Hermetic Order of the Golden Dawn was founded in the late 1800's. A. E. Waite in his otherwise excellent edition of the *Hermetic and Alchemical Writings of Paracelsus* (which was translated from the Latin of the 1658 Geneva folio) omits the *Archidoxes Magicae* along with other works by Paracelsus which have a magical content.

Curious pieces of lore which have been repeated by generations of Paracelsus' admirers can be traced back to this text. For example, the so-called 'trident of exorcism' illustrated on page 114 is in fact a lamen for the restoration of the 'member of generation'. It is to be made from a horseshoe, and in its original form is designed only to counteract the effect of witchcraft on potency, rather than to be used as a full scale magical weapon.

The planetary and zodiacal seals need not be limited to medical applications but will also serve as personal zodiacal lamens or as very effective talismans, provided the specific objective is introduced into the design of the appropriate seal, in the appropriate planetary hour.

It is important to remember that when calculating planetary hours the period from sunrise to sunset is divided by twelve to give the length of the hour, and the planets are then allocated in the order Saturn, Jupiter, Mars, Sun, Venus, Mercury, and Moon, commencing with the planet which rules the day in question. It is also worthwhile noting that when Paracelsus refers to the Sun entering Aries on the tenth day of March, that the procession of the equinoxes in the last five centuries has carried the date of the vernal equinox forward.

It remains to 'present the ingenious Reader with a part of the Workes of the renowned Paracelsus of the secrets of Alchymy, Occult Philosophy, and the wonderfull operation of the Celestial bodyes, in curing diseases by sigils and characters, made and applyed in fit elected times and seasons, and under their proper constellations, as the Author hath directed. . . .'

STEPHEN SKINNER
London 1975

PARACELSVS

Of the

Supreme MYSTERIES

OF

NATURE.

Of { The Spirits of the Planets.
{ Occult Philofophy.

The Magical, Sympathetical,
and Antipathetical CURE
of Wounds and Difeafes.

The Myfteries of the twelve
SIGNS of the ZODI-
ACK.

Englifhed by *R. Turner,*

φιλομαθής.

London, Printed by *J. C.* for *N. Brook* and
J. Harifon ; and are to be fold at their fhops
at the Angel in Cornhil, and the holy Lamb
neer the Eaft-end of *Pauls.* 1656.

To the worthily respected, and
his much honoured Friend,

Doctor *Trigge*, Doctor in
PHYSICK;

Robert Turner wisheth health and
happiness.

Honoured Sir,

He successful experi-
ence and large pra-
ctice which you have
had in the Operations
of *Nature*, (I mean in the practical part of *Physick*) hath in-
vited me to present this piece of
A 2   that

The Epiftle

that moft renowned *Phyfitian*
Paracelfus *to your Patronage*;
which I have endeavoured to
bring into a garbe fuitable, as
neer as I can, to our *Englifh fa-
fhion*; though perhaps it's not fo
finely accoutred, and dreffed A
la mode, *as to fuit with every
critical or captious Fancy* : But
*as this Author in his time was
too learned and fincere in the
method of his practice*, to fuit
*with general Sophiftry of the wil-
fully ignorant Conclave of Phy-
fitians*; fo I doubt not, but you
have met with fome Invectives
amongft our common Collegians,
who ground the greateft reafon

of

Dedicatory.

of their Recipes from a Galen's or a Pliny's *Probatum*: But as this famous Author made Reason and Experience his greatest Guide, so I am assured you do; and therefore valued not the Calumnies, Oppositions, and Obtrectations of his Adversaries. Sir, this little Treatise presents you with the rare secrets of Alchymy, and the miraculous Cures of Diseases by Sigils and Lamens, made in their proper seasons, and attributed to the nature of Celestial Bodies; which to many Ignorants seems impossible, and is by them vilified because not understood : I there-

fore

The Epistle

fore make bold to crave your pro-
tection ,   which may sufficiently
arm it against all Opposites. And
be pleased to pardon my boldness
herein, and admit of this my la-
bour into your Patronage ; that
your favourable acceptance here-
of may be a future encourage-
ment to

August 20.
1655.

Yours to

Command,

R. Turner.

To

To the READER.

Courteous Reader,

IN this laſt Iron age, ignorance hath ſo much pre-
vailed, that many have, and yet do plead for it, and
ſtrive to uphold it, crying down all Arts, and endea-
vouring to hood-wink knowledge; ſo that nothing but
the feces and dreggs of Art ſeems to remain: ſo that
they ſeem but ſhadows, if compared with that priſtine
learning of the Ancients. What golden Legends
formerly flouriſhed among the Hebrews, and Ægyp-
tians, and are now even almoſt all loſt in Oblivion?
But becauſe Babels confuſion is one great reaſon of
the decay of Sciences, which are not in every Mother-
tongue underſtood, and the diſpoſition of moſt people
of our times is to breed their children up better fed
then taught, their conditions are rather to pour into
the earth, Unde effodiuntur opes irritamenta ma-
lorum; then to look Heavenwards with that Os ſublime wherewith they were created: which the Poet
tells of, Ovid met,

Os homini ſublime dedit cœlumque videri juſ-
ſit, &c.

Whereas all beaſts look down with Groveling eye,
To man God gave looks mixt with Majeſty,
And will'd him with bold face to view the Sky.

To the Reader.

And therefore I present the ingenious Reader with a part of the Workes of the renowned Paracelsus *of the secrets of Alchymy, Occult Philosophy, and the wonderfull operation of the Celestial bodyes, in curing diseases by sigils and characters, made and applyed in fit elected times and seasons, and under their proper constellations, as the Author hath directed. I must expect the sottish Malignant censures of* Zoylus *and* Momus, *and such fools: but the Author himself in his Prologue in the ensuing discourse, sufficiently cleares all objections, and therefore I shall save that labour; onely I would have such men not be so wilfully ignorant, as altogether to forget, that the Heavens declare the glory of God, and the Firmament sheweth his handy-worke. Indeed* Mechanicks *and* Empiricks *do abuse all Arts : One* Mountebank *railes in verse against Astrology, and impudently calls the professors thereof cheaters,* (Sed seipsum intueri oportet) *and gives this to be his onely reason, that a fools bolt is soon shot ; and that he endeavoured to vilifie that Art, because he was altogether ignorant of it himself, and would gladly learn it ; but he knew not how nor which way to begin : another (and too many such render the Art vile) Poetizes upon the Art of Astrologie, and pretends to cure all diseases and know all things by it, and indeed knows nothing : such are a great Scandal to the excellency of such Sciences :* Sed non loquor stultis. *This translation is rendered rather Grammatically then Sententially, according to the Authors own phrase : shortly expect* (Deo volente) *the other parts hereof, and some comments on this and them, together with the famous art of Steganography,* Authore Tritemio, *to speak our*

own

To the Reader.

own *Language* ; *and perhaps the Occult Philosophy* of Agrippa *digested into a plainer method. this should have been now inlarged, but* prefens Status noster *is the reason, and the excuse the same as* Ovid's :

Nubila funt fubitis tempora noftra malis.

It is the General opinion of most ignorant people, to count all things that are above their Vulgar apprehenfions, to be diabolicall, and meerly brought to pafs by the works of the Devil: and under that notion they conclude all the fecret and Magnetick operations of nature, and thereby rob God the creator of all things, of that glory that is due unto him onely, and attribute the fame to the Devil, the enemy to God and all the world: I shall therefore here take occafion to tell fuch people (becaufe their Priefts, that should teach them knowledge, either cannot or elfe will not) what the Devil is. As in the Microcofmus or little world Man, the Soul is the beft part, and the excrements the worft; fo in the great world, as the Univerfal creating fpirit is the beft part, fo is the Devil the excrement of that Univerfal Spirit, and the abject and Caput mortuum *of the world ; and the pooreft and moft wretched of all created beings: And that worketh a great Antipathy between him and us, and the bleffed holy Angels, who are our Governors and Protectors, and continual guardians, and are continually employed about us, according to their orders and minifteries appointed them by the moft High : although the Devil alwayes endeavoureth to imitate and counterfeit the good Angels, and thereby deceiveth many whofe wickednefs and malice fuits with his nature, and at which the good Angel being grieved, leaves them ; and many times for the wickednefs of fome Perfon or Family, the*

good

To the Reader.

good *Angel curses such a person and family, or house;
then the wicked Spirit haunts such houses, affright-
ing the people with many fearful apparitions ; neither
can that house be quiet, nor any such person ; neither
shall any of the Generation of any such family prosper
untill that curse be expiated, and the angry Angel ap-
peased ; as this Author will tell you, and woful experience daily shews : how frequently, and familiar-
ly did those blessed Angels visibly communicate with
the holy men and Magicians of old ! though now such
is the wickedness of our age, that they have almost
quite forsaken us: although they are alwayes present
about us, though invisible, administring to us according to the orders given unto them from the second
Hierarchy, who receive the same from the first Hierarchy, who always attend before the Throne of the
divine Majesty, offering up the prayers of the Saints,
&c. If any one account this superstition, I hope I
shall never be of the Number of those who for fear of
being superstitious, have reformed themselves and
hunted Religion till they have lost the sent of it, into
meer Atheism and profaness. But lest I should di-
gresse* Ultra Crepidam, *and make a gate bigger then
the City, I will here conclude my self,* Esse idem qui
sum,

A Studio Divinæ
Contemplationis ,
Auguſt, 1655.

Robertus Turner.

In

In Commendation of his Friend's Translation.

THrice-welcome Paracelsus, most renown'd
Hermetick and Philosopher by fire,
Now in an English garb thou comest crown'd,
What need we for our Chymistry soar higher?
Since thou reveal'st with thy Prophetick Pen,
All's needful to be known by th' Sons of Men.
And thou, my noble Friend, who thus hast drest
Him in our English Fashion, dost deserve,
With Laurel to be crowned with the rest
Of those who dayly do Urania serve.   (fret,
Let wry-mouthed Cynicks, prate, preach, foam, and
Hermes true Sons will not thy love forget.
    Fare ever well, so ever wishes he
    Who is more yours, then he can seem to be.

W. F.

Astrophilus.

An

An Encomium upon his Friend the Translator's elaborate pains.

*F*Ly Galen *hence,* Hippocrates *be gone* ;
  I will preserve my choice : this is that One,
Whose true Elixir doth preserve the frame
Of Man's frail Nature, vivifies the same ;
By heavenly constellated Medicine,
Which vulgars count but Dross, I count Divine.
Let Zoil's *and* Momus *'s intoxicated brains*
Dispraise the Author 's works ; Translator *'s pains*
I'll foster, cherish with undaunted part
This true sublime Spagyrick noble Art.
  Proceed then, Friend, make all speak English : why
  Should we be barr'd our Native Liberty ?

W. Ryves,

Philomedicus.

The

The Contents of this Book.

To

The Contents.

                                                            Ta

The Contents.

Of

The Contents.

To be sold by *N.Brook* at the Angel in Cornhil,
A Romance called *The Imperious Brother,*
and *The Illustrious Shepherdess.*
Wit and Drollery : with other Jovial
Poems.

The Prologue.

Aving first invocated the Name of the Lord Jesus Christ our Saviour, we will enterprize this Work ; wherein we shall not only teach how to change any inferiour Metal into better, as Iron into Copper, this into Silver, and that into Gold, &c. but also to help all infirmities, whose cure to the opinionated and presumptuous Physitians, doth seem impossible : But that which is greater, to preserve, and keep mortal men to a long, sound, and perfect Age. This A R T was by our Lord God the Supream Creator, ingraven as it were in a book in the body of Metals, from the beginning of the Creation, that we might diligently learn from them. Therefore when any

man

man defireth throughly and perfectly to
learn this Art from its true foundation, it
will be neceffary that he learn the fame
from the Mafter thereof, to wit, from
God, who hath created all things, and
onely knoweth what Nature and Propriety he himfelf hath placed in every Creature. Wherefore he is able to teach e-
very one certainly and perfectly : and
from him we may learn abfolutely, as he
hath fpoken, faying, *Of me ye fhall learn*
all things : for there is nothing found in
Heaven nor in Earth fo fecret, whofe properties he perceiveth not, and moft exactly knoweth and feeth, who hath created
all things. We will therefore take him to
be our Mafter, Operator, and Leader into
this moft true Art. We will therefore imitate him alone, and through him learn and
attain to the knowledge of that Nature,
which he himfelf with his own finger hath
engraven and infcribed in the bodies of
thefe Metals. Hereby it will come to pafs,
that the moft high Lord God fhall blefs all
the Creatures unto us, and fhall fanctifie
all our Wayes ; fo that in this Work we
may be able to bring our Beginning to its
defired End, and the Confequence thereof
to

upon Nature it felf, and upon thofe Vertues and Powers, which GOD with his own Finger hath impreffed in Metals. Of this impreffion *Mercurius Trifmegiftus* was an Imitator, who is not undefervedly called the Father of all Wife-men, and of all thofe that followed this ART with love, and with earneft defire, and that man demonftrateth and teacheth, that God alone is the onely author, caufe and Original of all creatures in this ART. But he doth not attribute the power and virtue of God, to the creatures or vifible things, as the faid heathen, and fuch-like did. Now feeing all ART ought to be learned from the Trinity;that is,from God the Father, from God the Son of God, our Saviour Jefus Chrift, and from God the holy Ghoft, three diftinct perfons, but one God: We will therefore divide this our Alchymiftical worke into three parts, or Treatifes:in the firft whereof, we will lay down what the ART containeth in it felf; And what is the propriety and nature of every Metal: Secondly, by what means a man may worke and bring the like powers and ftrength of Metals to effect. And thirdly, what Tinctures are to be produced from the Sun and Moone.   Pato produce exceeding great Joy and Love in our Hearts.

But if any one shall follow his own onely Opinion, he will not onely greatly deceive himself; but also all others who cleave and adhere thereunto; and shall bring them unto loss. For mankinde is certainly born in ignorance, so that he can neither know nor understand any thing of himself; but onely that which he receiveth from God, and understandeth from Nature. He which learneth nothing from these, is like the Heathen Masters and Philosophers, who follow the Subtilties and Crafts of their own Inventions and Opinions, such as are *Aristotle*, *Hippocrates*, *Avicenna*, *Gallen*, &c. who grounded all their ARTS upon their own Opinions onely. And if at any time they learned any thing from Nature, they destroyed it again with their own Phantasies, Dreams, or Inventions, before they came to the end thereof; so that by them and their Followers there is nothing perfect at all to be found.

This therefore hath moved and induced us hereunto, to write a peculiar book of Alchymy, founded not upon men, but
upon

Paracelſus

Of the Secrets of ALCHYMY;
Diſcovered, in the Nature of the PLANETS.

CHAP. I.

Of ſimple Fire.

N the firſt place, we ſhall endeavour and undertake to declare, what this Art comprehendeth, and what is the ſubjeƈt thereof; and what are its proprieties.

The prime and chief ſubjeƈt to this Art belonging, is fire; which always liveth in one and the ſame propriety and o-

B 3   pera-

peration; neither can it receive life from any thing elſe. Wherefore it hath a condition and power, as all fires that lie hid in ſecret things, have, of vivification, no otherwiſe then the Sun is appointed of God, which heateth all the things of the world, both ſecret, apparent & manifeſt; as the Spheres of *Mars, Saturn, Venus, Jupiter, Mercury,* and *Luna,* which can give no other light but what they borrow from the Sun, for they are dead of themſelves. Neverthelefs, when they are kindled, as above is ſpoken, they worke and operate according to their properties. But the Sun himſelf receiveth his light from no other but from God himſelf, who ruleth him by himſelf, ſo that he burneth and ſhineth in him. It is no otherwiſe in this art. The fire in the furnace is compared to the Sun, which heateth the furnace and the veſſels, as the Sun in the great world; for even as nothing can be brought forth in the world without the Sun, ſo likewiſe in this Art nothing can be produced without this Simple fire; no operation can be made without it: it is the greateſt ſecret of this Art; comprehending all things which are comprehended therein, neither can it be comprehended in any elſe; for it abideth by it ſelf: it lacketh nothing; but other things which want that, do injoy it, and have life from it; wherefore we have in the firſt place undertooke to declare it.

Chap.

CHAP. II.

Of the multiplicity of fire, from which varieties of Metalls do arise.

WE have firſt written of ſimple fire which liv-eth and ſubſiſteth of it ſelf: now we come to ſpeake of a manifold ſpirit or fire, which is the cauſe of variety and diverſity of creatures, ſo that there cannot one be found right like ano-ther, and the ſame in every part; as it may be ſeen in Metals, of which there is none which hath another like it ſelf: the *Sun* produceth his gold; the *Moon* produceth another Metal far diffe-rent, to wit, ſilver; *Mars* another, that is to ſay, Iron; *Jupiter* produceth another kind of Metal, to wit, Tin; *Venus* another, which is Copper; and *Saturn* another kind, that is to ſay, Lead: ſo that they are all unlike, and ſeveral one from ano-ther: the ſame appeareth to be as well amongſt men as all other creatures, the cauſe whereof is the multiplicity of fire.   As by ſome heat is produced a mean generation by the corruption thereof; the waſhing of the Sea another, Aſhes another, Sand another, Flame of fire another, and another of Coales, &c.   This variety of creatures is not made of the firſt ſimple fire, but of the regiment of elements, which is various; not from the Sun, but from the courſe of the ſeven Planets.   And this is the reaſon that the

world

world containeth nothing of ſimilitude in its
individuals : for as the heat is altered and changed every hour and minute;ſo alſo all other things
are varyed : for the tranſmutation of the fire is
made in the elements, in which bodies it is im-
printed by this fire. Where there is no great
mixture of the elements, the Sun bringeth forth ;
where it is a little more thicke, the *Moon*;
where more groſs, *Venus :* and thus according to
the diverſity of mixtures, are produced divers
Metals ; ſo that no Metal appeareth in the ſame
mine like another. It is therefore to be known,
that this variety of Metals is made of the mixture
of the Elements, becauſe that their ſpirits are alſo found divers and without ſimilitude ; which if
they were brought forth from the ſimple fire, they
would be ſo like , that one could not be known
from another. but the manifold variety of forms
interceding , hath introduced the ſame among
the creatures. From this it may eaſily be gathered, why ſo many and ſo various forms of Metals
are found, and wherefore there is none like unto another.

Chap. III.

Of the ſpirit or tin[[ture of ☉.

NOw we come to the ſpirits of the Planets
or Metals. The ſpirit or tincture of the *Sun*
taketh its beginning from a pure, ſubtil, and perfect fire; whereby it cometh to paſs,that it far excelleth

celleth all other fpirits and tinƐures of Metals:
for it remaineth conftantly fixed in the fire , out
of which it flyeth not ; neither is it confumed
thereby, much lefs burnt , but rather appeareth
more cleere, faire and pure by it; alfo no heat
nor cold can hurt it, nor no other accident, as
in the other fpirits or tinƐures of Metals: and
for this caufe, the body which it once putteth
on, it defendeth from all accidents and difeafes,
that it may be able to fuftain the fire without detriment. This body hath not this power and
virtue in it felf, but from the fpirit of the Sun
which is included therein : for we know that the
Sun is the body of *Mercury* , and that this body
cannot fuftain nor fuffer this fire, but flyeth from
it ; when as it doth not fly from the fire when it
is in the Sun, but remaineth conftant and fixed
therein. This affordeth unto us a moft certain
Judgement , that it receiveth fuch a conftancy
from his fpirit or tinƐure: wherefore if that fpirit
can be in this *Mercury,* every one may judge
that it may worke the fame in the bodies of
men , when it is received of them ; as we
have fufficiently fpoken in our *Magna Chirur-
gia,* of the tinƐure of the *Sun,* that it will not
onely reftore and preferve them that ufe it, from
infirmities , but alfo preferve them to found and
long life. In like manner, the ftrength & virtues of
all other Metals are to be known from true experience, not from the wifdom of men and of the
world, which is foolifhnefs with God & his truth;
and all thofe who do build upon that wifdom,
and repofe their hope thereupon are miferably
deceived.   Chap.

___

CHAP. IV.

Of the tincture and Spirit of the ☽.

HAving now ſpoken of the tincture of the
Sun, it remaineth that we come now to ſpeak of
the tincture of the *Moon*, and of the white tincture, which is alſo created of a perfect ſpirit,
but leſs perfect then the ſpirit of the *Sun*. Nevertheleſs it excelleth the tinctures of all other
Metals following, both in purity & ſubtilty; which
is very well known to all that treat of the *Moon*,
and alſo to Ruſticks: for it ſuffereth not ruſt, nei-
their is it conſumed by the fire ; as all other
Metals, as *Saturn*, which fly from the fire ; but
this doth not: from whence it may be gathered,
that this tincture is far more excellent then the
other following, for it preſerveth its body that
it aſſumeth conſtantly in the fire, without any
accident or detriment : and from hence it is ſufficiently manifeſt, if this in his own corruptible
body by himſelf maketh *Mercury*, what will it
be able to effect, being extracted from it ſelf into
another body ? will not that alſo ſave and defend
from infirmities and accidents after the ſame
manner ? Yes ſurely, if it make this *Mercury* in
its own body, it will do the ſame in the bodies of
men : neither doth it onely preſerve health,
but cauſeth long life, and cureth diſeaſes and infirmities, even in thoſe who ſubſiſt beyond
the

the ordinary courſe of nature : for the more high, ſubtile and perfect the medicine is, ſo much the better and more perfectly it cureth : wherefore they are Ignorant Phyſitians, who practice their Art onely upon vegetables, as herbs and ſuch-like things, which are eaſily corrupted: and by theſe, they endeaour to effect & bring to paſs ſuch workes as are firme and ſtable ; but in vain, whenas they occupy the Aire. But wherefore ſhould we ſpeake much concerning theſe ? They never learned any better things in their Univerſities : therefore if they have been compelled ſo to learn and ſtudy from their beginning, they think it a great diſgrace to them to do otherwiſe for the future : whereby it comes to paſs, that they ſtill continue in their old Ignorance.

Chap. V.

Of the ſpirit of ♀.

WE have even now made mention of a white ſpirit, or candid tincture: now we come to ſpeake of a Red ſpirit, which is derived out of a Groſs Elementary mixture of the ſuperiours, to which alſo it is joyned, & is of a more perfect ſubſtance, then the ſpirits and tinctures of the other ſubſequent Metals, becauſe it endureth the fire longer then the other, and is not ſo ſoon melted or diſſolved as the other ſpirits which follow. Alſo the ayre, and the humidity of the fire, are

not

not fo nocent unto it, as unto *Mars*; by reafon whereof, it doth the longer endure the fire. This power and property hath *Venus*, that is his body, from the fpirit that is infufed into it.   Now the fame effect that it worketh in its own body, that is, in *Venus*, the fame effects it alfo produceth in the bodies of men, fo far forth as nature hath granted unto it; for it preferveth wounds in fuch manner, fo that no accident can invade them, nor the Air or water hurt them ;   and expelleth all fuch difeafes as are under the degree thereof.   This fpirit alfo breaketh the bodies of Metals, fo that they will endure the hammer ; and alfo in the bodies of men, when it is taken of them with whom it agreeth not, it effecteth things not convenient. Wherefore it is very neceffary, that the Phyfician that defires to make ufe of thefe fpirits, be very expert in the knowledge of Metals. Therefore it is far better to ufe the more perfect fpirits, which may be taken without any fuch feare of danger: neverthelefs, feeing the fpirits of the *Sun* and *Moon* are dear and precious, fo that every one is not able to accomplifh them, to perform cures with , therefore every one muft take according to his ability , what he is able to attain unto : alfo every one is not fo wealthy, that he can be able to prepare thefe medicines ; therefore he is forced to take fuch as he can have. Every one may from hence eafily gather, that the Metallike medicines do far exceed vegetables and Animals in ftrength and power of curing and healing. And thus-much of the fpirit of *Venus*.

Chap.

CHAP. VI.

Of the Spirit of ♂.

THat we may now come to fpeake of the Spirit of *Mars*, that is of a more Grofs and combuftible mixture of Elements, then the other fpirits going before; but the Spirit of *Mars* is endued with a greater hardnefs then the other Metals; fo that it doth not fo eafily melt and diffolve in the fire, as the other following. But it fuffers much hurt both by the water and the Aire, fo that it is confumed by them, and is burnt with the fire, as experience makes appeare: Wherefore the Spirit thereof is more imperfect then any of the fuperiour fpirits: but in hardnefs and drynefs it exceedeth all other Metals, both fuperiour and inferiour : for it doth not onely retain a perfect fubftance, and refift the hammer, as the *Sun* and *Moon*, but alfo as thofe which are within it felf, as *Jupiter* and *Saturn*, and the like. Whereas therefore it thus worketh in Metals, it fheweth that it hath the fame effect in the bodies of men, that is, it produceth reluctancy; efpecially where it is taken for a difeafe not convenient, it grievoufly afflicteth the members with pain. Neverthelefs, when it is taken and applyed for wounds, fuch as do not exceed its own degree, it cleanfeth and mundifieth them, &c. Wherefore this fpirit is not much lefs in power and virtue then one of the fuperiours, in thofe things for which it was by God and Nature ordained. Chap.

CHAP. VII.

Of the Spirit of ♃.

OF the ſpirit of *Jupiter*, we are to know, that
it is derived of a white and pale ſubſtance of
fire; but it is of a frangible and brittle nature, not
enduring the hammer, ſo as *Mars:* wherefore it is
a brittle Metal : an example thereof appears, if
it be mixed with the *Moon*, it can hardly be
wrought to its firſt malleation, without great labour : the ſame effect it hath in all other Metals,
except in *Saturn* onely. And the ſame operation
which it hath in the bodies of metals, it alſo
produceth the ſame effects in humane bodies; but
burneth & corrodeth the members, hindring them
from their own perfect operations, thereby diſa-
bling them form performing the work which nature requires, & neceſſitates them unto. Nevertheleſs, this ſpirit hath in it this virtue, that it taketh away the ulcers of cancers, fiſtula's and ſuch
like, eſpecially ſuch as exceed not. the degree of
its nature which God and Nature have given
unto it.

Chap.

CHAP. VIII.

Of the Spirit of ♄.

THe Spirit of *Saturn* is formed and created of a dry, cold and blacke mixture of the Elements; whereby it comes to pafs, that amongft all other Metals, it endureth leaft in the fire : Whereas the *Sun* and *Moon* are proved to be durable : if *Saturn* be added to them, it clearly refineth them; neverthelefs the nature thereof is to diminifh their hardnefs. The fame operation it hath in the bodies of men, but with great pain and dolour, as *Jupiter* and *Mars*, by reafon of the mixture that it hath with the cold, wherefore it cannot fo mildly operate. But it hath great power and vertue in the cures of fiftula's, cancers and ulcers, which are under the degree and nature thereof: it expelleth outward difeafes, and the outward impurities of the *Moon*. Neverthelefs if it be not carefully applyed, it doth more hurt then good; wherefore he that would rightly ufe it, ought neceffarily to know the nature thereof, and what difeafes it cureth, and may be applyed unto: which being neceffarily confidered, no hurt will follow thereby

Chap.

Chap. IX.

Of the Groſs Spirit of ☿.

THe Spirit of *Mercury*, which is onely
ſubjected to the other ſuperiour Spirits,
hath no certain determinate form or ſubſtance in it ſelf: hereby it comes to paſs that it
admitteth every other Metal: even as wax receiveth the impreſſion of all forms of Seales, ſo this
Elementary Spirit cometh to be compared to the
other Spirits of Metals : for if it receive into it
ſelf the Spirit of the *Sun* , this ſhall be made
out of it ſelf;if the *Moon*,ſhe is made out of it ſelf:
the ſame effect this Spirit worketh with all the
other Metals with whom it agreeth,and receiveth
their properties into it ſelf: for this cauſe,accord-
ing to its body, it is appropriated to the other
Spirits above written, even as the Male to the
Female: for the Sun is the body of *Mercury*, except onely that the Sun faſtneth and fixeth the
Mercury;but the common *Mercury* is inconſtant
and volatile: neverthelefs it is ſubject to all the
Spirits aforeſaid, and generateth again, not onely the metallicke Spirits and tinctures afore
ſpoken of, but the Metal it ſelf, by which the
aforenamed tinctures do come into their operation : But if the mean be not obſerved,it will be
inpoſſible ever to bring thoſe kind of tinctures
to perfection : for if the fire be too high which
                                                      ſhould

should vivifie this tincture, it doth extinguish it, that it cannot operate; and the same effect is, if it be too weake: wherefore in this place it is necessary to be known what medium is to be observed in this Art, and what are the strength and properties thereof; and also after what manner it is to be ordered, and how the tinctures are to be coloured, and to bring them to a perfect worke, that they may germinate and appeare. Thus briefly do we conclude and end our first Treatise.

The end of the first Treatise.

C   *The*

The ſecond Treatiſe; of the Philoſophers *Mercury*, and the medium of Tinctures.

In the firſt Treatiſe we have written of the Spirits and Tinctures of Metals , &c. Declaring all their properties and natures, and what every Metal generateth. In this ſecond, we ſhall treat of the medium of Tinctures, that is, of the Philoſophers Mercury ; whereby are made the Tinctures and Leaven of Metals, in ſeven Chapters following.

CHAP. I.

Of what the Tinctures and Leavens are made.

WHoſoever deſireth to have the tincture of Metals , he ought to take the Philoſophers *Mercury*, & let him caſt the ſame into its own end, that is, into quick *Mercury*, from whence it proceedeth; & hereby it wil come to paſs , that the Philoſophers *Mercury* ſhall be diſſolved in the quick *Mercury*, and ſhall receive its ſtrength : ſo that the *Mercury* of the Philoſophers killeth the quick *Mercury*, & maketh it remain fixed in the fire of the ſame exiſtence with it ſelf : for there is the like concordancy between theſe *Mercuries*, as is between Male and Female,

man

man and wife ; for they are both derived of the
grofs fpirits of metals, except that the body of *Sol*
remaineth firm & fixed in the fire: but the quicke
Mercury is not fixed ; neverthelefs they may be
appropriated one to another, as graine of corn or
feed are to the earth ; which we will demon-
ftrate by an example, after this manner : If any
one fowe barley, the fame he fhall reape ; if
Wheat or Rye, or any other grain, the fame he
fhall gather,&c.even fo it is in this art;if any one
fowe the Gold of *Sol*, the fame he reapeth ; & of
the *Moon*,he fhall gather; and fo alfo of all other
Metals. For this reafon we fay in this place, that
the Tinctures do fpring out of Mettals, that is,
out of the Philofophers *Mercury*, and not from
the quicke *Mercury* ; but this produceth the Seed
which firft conceiveth.

CHAP. II.

*Of the Conjunction of Male and Female, of man and
woman.*

IT is firft of all neceffary to be known,that the
Mercury of the Philofophers, and the quicke
Mercury, are both to be conjoyned and firmly
united and fixed together ; how much thereof is to be taken: neither more nor lefs then
equal, is to be taken, left it hindreth, or altogether deftroyeth the whole worke ; For the
feed is fuffocated with fuperfluity, that it cannot
live fo long until it be joyned and fixed to the

Philoſophers *Mercury*. But if there be too little,
that it cannot be diſſolved into a body, it is alſo
deſtroyed, that it cannot be able to bring forth
any fruit: wherefore the Artificer ought certainly
to know how much of the one, and the other
ought to be taken, if he would bring this
worke to its perfect end; the Receipt thereof
is this: Take one part to two, or three to four,
and thou canſt not erre, but ſhalt attain to thy
deſired end.

<hr>

CHAP. III.

Of the form of the Inſtruments of Glaſs.

THe Materials being thus rightly and duly
prepared and mixt together, then you muſt
have Glaſs-veſſels, of due proportion, and even
fitneſs and capacity; neither too great nor too
little, but fit: For if the veſſels be too big, the
Female, that is, the flegme, is diſperſed and loſt;
whereby it comes to paſs that the ſeed cannot
bring forth: where the veſſels are too little,
the growth is ſuffocated that it cannot come to
fruit, no otherwiſe but as if ſeed ſhould be ſowne
under trees or under thornes, ſo that it cannot
bud and ſpring up, but periſheth without any
fruit; therefore no little error may happen by
the veſſels; which being once committed, cannot
be any more mended in the ſame worke: neither can that worke be perfected or brought to
any

any good end. Wherefore, note what follows, to wit, that you take three ounces with the half, and four pounds ; fo the proceeding is right, and you fhall preferve the matter that it be not difperfed, nor the Phlegme nor the generation impedited, &c.

CHAP. IV.

Of the properties of the fire.

WHen you have placed the matter in fit veffels, you fhall carefully keep and maintain the natural heat, that the externall heat do not overcome or abound over the internal ; for if the heat be too much, there can be no conjunction made, by reafon that the matter is difperfed and burnt by the vehemency of the heat, fo that no good arifeth thereby. Wherefore the middle region of the air is by nature ordained between heaven and earth; otherwife the Sun and Stars would burn up all the creatures upon the earth, fo that nothing could be produced or fpring forth from it : therefore fo work, that you put fuch an Airy part or diftance between the matter and the fire ; after this manner let it be done, that the heat may not eafily do hurt any wayes, nor difperfe the matter, much - lefs burn it : but if the fire be too little, and not quick enough, the Spirit then refteth, the fire nothing operating upon its humidity; neither will it be exficcated nor fixed :

C 3   for

for the Spirits of Metals are dead of themſelves,
and do reſt, ſo that they cannot at all operate of
themſelves, unleſs they are quickned by the fire.
It is no otherwiſe in the great Univerſe of the
world, where ſeed being caſt into the earth, is
dead, and cannot grow nor increaſe of it ſelf,
unleſs it be quickned by the heat of the Sun; It
is chiefly neceſſary therefore in this worke, to
erect and build the fire right and proportion-
ably, neither too great nor too little; otherwiſe this worke will never be brought to a perfect and deſired end.

CHAP. V.

Of the Signes appearing in the union of Conjunction.

THe fire being moderately kept & maintained,
the matter by little and little will be moved
to blackneſs; afterwards, when the dryneſs begins to worke upon the humidity, there will
likewiſe ariſe in the Glaſs, various flowers of
divers colours, ſuch as appeare like the taile of a
Peacocke, and ſuch as no man ever ſaw before.
Alſo ſomtimes the Glaſs appeareth as if it were
almoſt drawn into Gold; which being perceived,
it ſheweth certainly that the ſeed of the Male
doth rule and operate upon the ſeed of the Female, and that the ſame is fixed together; that
is, this *Mercury* is fixed and worketh upon the
quick *Mercury*, and beginneth to be mixed with
it

it: afterwards, when the humidity begins to weare away by the drynefs, thofe colours do difperfe, and the matter then beginneth at length to wax white, and fo proceedeth until it come to the higheft degree of whitenefs. But efpecially it is to be noted, that the thing is not to be haftened, according to their opinions who fuppofe fuch work to be like unto that which is difcerned in the production of corn, and of mankind; to wit, the time of bringing forth the one, is in the Space of nine moneths; the other, ten or twelve moneths. For fo foon the Sun and **Moon** do caufe Maturity, and bring to the birth, as the infant from the belly of his Mother; fo the grain from the bowells of the earth. For it is to be known, that every thing that is quickly or haftily made or born, doth foon perifh: An example hereof, both men & herbs do afford. They which are fooneft produced or born, their life is fhort: it is not fo with the *Sun* and *Moon*; for they caufe a far more perfect nature in men ; whereby it comes to pafs, that they produce long life to them, and preferve them from many accidents and difeafes.

CHAP. VI.

Of the knowledge of the perfect Tincture

IN the foregoing chapter, we have fet forth how the matter it felf worketh by degrees : but in

C4　　　　　　　this

this, we ſhall declare, by what means it may be known when it is perfect. Thus do: take the white ſtone of the *Moon*, by which the white ſpringeth, and ſeparate a little peece from it with a paire of Sciſſars, and put it upon a plate of Copper, heating it glowing hot in the fire: if it ſmoke, then the ſtone is not perfect, therefore it muſt remain longer in the decoction, until the ſtone come to its degree of perfection: but if it do not ſmoke, then be aſſured it is perfect: the ſame is to be done with the Red ſtone of the *Sun*, in the degrees of the operation thereof.

Chap. VII.
To Augment or Multiply the Tinctures.

VVHen you would Multiply or increaſe the Tincture you have found, mixt it together again with common *Mercury*, and worke it in all things as at firſt, and double one part a hundred times more then it was coloured before; this do often-times over again, until you have as much matter as you will: and by how much the longer it remaineth in the fire, by ſo much the higher and more ſublime will the degrees thereof be; ſo that one part thereof will change the infinity of the quick *Mercury*, into the beſt and moſt perfect *Luna* and *Sol*. Now you have the whole progreſſion from the beginning to the end; wherewith we end this ſecond Treatiſe, and begin the third.

The end of the ſecond Treatiſe.   In

In the second Treatise, we have told how the Tinctures or Leavens ought to be made ; in the third, we shall declare and amply set forth wherewith the Tinctures of the Sun and Moon are made ; and after what manner Sol *and the other Planets ought to be made ; to wit, with the Furnace and the Fire.*

Chap. I.

Of the building of the Furnace ; and, of the Fire.

MErcurius Hermes Trifmegiftus, faith, That he which would perfect this Art, muft, as it were, build a new World ; for after the fame manner as God created the Heaven and Earth, the Furnace with the Fire is to be built and governed. That is to fay, after this manner: Firft, Let there be a Furnace built of the height of fix fpans, extended from the top of the fingers to the thumb ; and in breadth one handful ; in the infide, let it be round and plain, left the Coals cleave unto it ; from whence let it a little decline to the border thereof ; and let there be holes left underneath

four

four fingers broad, and let every hole of the Furnace be fupplied with a Copper Cauldron to contain the Water.   Afterwards, take good and hard Coals, which you fhall break in Gobbets about the bignefs of a Walnut; with thefe fill the long Furnace; which then is to be ftopped up, that they may not burn out.   And afterwards, let fome Coals be kindled to the holes below: if the Fire be too great, lay a ftone before it; if too little, ftir the Coals with an Iron-inftrument, that they may be pierced with the Air, and the Heat may be increafed. This way you may keep your Fire, according to the true Exigency of Nature; neither too exceffive, nor too fmall; but moft fit and apt for the motion of the Matter: this is compared to the Firmament.   There is alfo in this place another Firmament, to wit, the Matter contained in the Glafs; after which followeth the form of the World.   Therefore the Furnace is to be placed as the Sun in the great World, which giveth Light, Life and Heat to the univerfal Furnace, and all Inftruments, and to all other things whatfoever concluded under it.

Chap.

CHAP. II.

Of the Conjunction of the Male with the Female.

HAving now treated of the Furnace and the
Fire wherein the Tinctures are to be prepared, now we intend largely to write how the
Man and Woman do agree , and how they are
joyned together: that is to say , after this manner : Take the *Mercury* of the Philosophers, prepared and mundified in its highest degree ; this
resolve with his Wife, to wit, with quick *Mercury*; as the Woman receiveth the Man, and as
the Man cleaveth to the Woman : and even as a
Man loveth his Wife, and the Woman loveth her
Husband , so do the Philosophers *Mercury* and
the quick *Mercury* , prosecute the greatest love,
and are moved by Nature with a great affection
towards us : So therefore the one and the other
Mercuries are conjoyned each to other, and one
with another, even as the Man with the Woman,
and she with him, according to their bodies, that
there is no difference between them;and they are
congruent in their strength and proprieties, save
onely, that the Man is firm and fixed , but the
Woman is volatile in the Fire. And for this
Cause , the Woman is united.to the Man, so
that she receiveth the Man, and he fixeth and
fastneth her firm and constant in any balance ;
as it followeth, They are both to be so close
luted

luted and covered, that the Woman may not e-
vaporate or breath out, otherwiſe the whole
Work will come to nothing.

Chap. III.

Of the Copulation of the Male and Female.

VVHen you have placed the Man and the
Wife in the Matrimonial Bed ; if you
would that he may operate upon her, ſo that
ſhe may bring forth , it is neceſſary, and muſt be,
that the Man have his operation upon the Woman, ſo that the ſeed of the Woman may be co-
agulated and joyned together into a Maſs, by the
ſeed of the Man; otherwiſe it produceth no
Fruit.

Chap. IV.

Of the Philoſophical conjunction of the Man and Wo-man.

AFterwards if you perceive the Woman
to be of a black colour, then certainly be
aſſured that ſhe hath conceived, and is made
pregnant : and when the ſeed of the Woman
embraceth the ſeed of the Man, this is the firſt
Signe and Key of this whole Art ; therefore be
care-

careful continually to preserve the natural Heat, and the blackness will appear, and be disperfed and confumed away by the natural Heat; as one Worm eateth and devoureth another, and continueth confuming fo long, until there be no more blackness left.

CHAP. V.

Of the black Colour.

THe blackness manifeftly appearing, then know, that the Woman is pregnant ; but when the Peacocks Tail begins to appear,that is, when many various colours will appear in the Glafs,it fheweth the working of the Philofophers *Mercury* upon the vulgar *Mercury,*and ftretcheth out her Wings until fhe hath overcome it.Therefore when the drinefs operates upon the moifture, thefe Colours do appear.

CHAP. VI.

Of the Buds fpringing and appearing in the Glafs.

VVHen you perceive thefe various Colours, then be conftant in your work, continuing the Fire, until the Colour of the Peacock's Tail be fully confumed, and until the Matter of
the

the *Moon* appear white and candid as Snow, and that the Veſſel hath brought it to the very degree of its perfection. Then at laſt break a little piece thereof, and put it on a Copper-plate in the Fire; if it remain conſtant and firm, and keep its Tincture, it is then brought to the moſt perfect ſubſtance of *Luna*. This King hath ſtrength and power, not onely to tranſmute and change all metals; but alſo to cure all diſeaſes and infirmities.   This King is laudable, and adorned with many vertues, and with ſo great power, that he can tranſmute and change *Venus*, *Mars*, *Jupiter*, *Saturn*, and *Mercury*, into the moſt conſtant *Luna*, to every touch-ſtone;   and alſo frees and delivers the bodies of men from infinite diſeaſes, as from Fevours, Feebleneſs, Leproſie, the French diſeaſe, or *Morbus Gallicus*, and from a great many other infirmities and diſeaſes; which no Herbs, Roots, or the like Medicines can poſſibly Cure, or take away. Whoſoever maketh daily uſe of this Medicine, ſhall attain to, and preſerve himſelf in a ſound and perfect long life.

Chap. VII.
Of the red Colour.

AFter this King is indued with a perfect whiteneſs, the Fire is conſtantly to be continued, until the whiteneſs begins to take a yellow Colour; which Colour follows next after the whiteneſs: for by how much the longer the Heat worketh upon the white and dry

Mat-

Matter, the more Yellow and Saffron-like groweth the Colour, until it come to perfect redness,
which by degrees the Fire worketh to the highest
degree of the red Colour; then is the substance
of Gold prepared, and there is born an oriental
King, sitting in his Throne, and ruling over all
the Princes of the World.

CHAP. VIII.

Of the augmentation or multiplication hereof.

THe multiplication of this Matter is to be after this manner, to wit, let it be resolved
into its moisture, and then put the Fire to it, to
the height as at first, and it will work upon its
moisture oftner then before, and change the same
into its own substance, turning the whole quantity of the matter into the substance it self: wherefore the Treasures of the Earth are unspeakable,
the world cannot compare unto them; witness
Augurellus.

The Conclusion.

This secret was kept by the most ancient Fathers amongst their most occult and hidden secrets; who kept the same, lest it should come to
the hands of wicked men, who might thereby be
inabled the better, and more fully to accomplish
their wickedness and evil ends. We therefore do
require you whosoever shall attain to this gift of
God, that you will imitate the Fathers, and se-
cretly

cretly uſe and preſerve this divine Myſtery : for if you tread it under your feet, or caſt Pearls before ſwine ; you ſhall receive a great judgement from God the great Judge and Revenger of all things.

But unto thoſe whom God by his ſingular and ſpecial Grace, hath given abſtinency from all vices, this Art ſhall be more fully revealed then to any other ; for with one ſuch man ſhall more wiſdom be found, then among a thouſand ſons of the world, by whom this Art ſhall never be found out.

Whoſoever ſhall finde out this ſecret, and attain to this gift of God, let him praiſe the moſt high God, the Father, Son, and Holy Ghoſt ; the Grace of God let him onely implore, that he may uſe the ſame to his glory, and the profit of his Neighbour. This the merciful God grant to be done, through Jeſus Chriſt his onely Son our Lord, *Amen.*

The

Theophraſtus Paracelſus
OF
OCCULT PHILOSOPHY.

The Prologue.

N this enſuing booke
we do intend to treat
of the greateſt and
moſt occult ſecrets of
Philoſophy, and of all
thoſe things which do
appertain to Magicke,
Nigromancy, Necro-
mancy, Pyromancy, Hydromancy, and Geomancy: Clearely and fully demonſtra-
ting
D

ting and setting forth every thing that may be investigated, effected and brought to pass thereby : this Philosophy in the practice thereof is much abused, by Ceremonies and other abuses ; and hitherto the foundation thereof hath been built falsely upon the sand ; whereby the whole Artifice and instruments thereof are overthrowne with the least winde, and sometimes the Artificers themselves, especially the Nigromancers, are taken away out of the very middest thereof, with the windes, that is, with the Spirits, and are vanquished, overcome and carryed away. It is therefore necessary that the foundation of these and of all other Arts be laid in the holy Scriptures, upon the doctrine and faith of Christ ; which is the most firme and sure foundation, and the chiefe corner stone, whereupon the three principal points of this Philosophy are grounded. The first is prayer, whereunto agrees this word of holy Scripture, *Ask, seeke, and knocke,* &c. By which we are to seeke unto God, and faithfully believe his promises; and doing this with a pure heart and minde, it shall be given unto us, and we shall finde what we seeke after : and those

thofe things which before remained occult
and fecret, fhall be made open and ma-
nifefted unto us. The fecond thing founded therein, is faith, which is able to remove Mountains into the Sea: for unto
the faithful all things are poffible, as
Chrift hath fpoken. The third point is
founded in our imagination, which after-
ward is kindled in our hearts, and then
aptly agreeth and concordeth with the
faith aforefaid.

Therefore all Ceremonies, Conjurations, Confecrations, and fuch like vanities
are to be rejected and caft away, with all
vain foundations, & the true corner-ftone
is the foundation that is onely to be im-
braced in our hearts, that is, every thing
which proceedeth and fpringeth from
the holy Scriptures, the light of nature,
and fountain of truth: we will write
therefore in moft briefe and plain words,
the moft occult and fecret things, which
neither *Cornelius Agrippa* nor *Peter de
Abano*, much lefs *Tritemius*, never underftood or wrote of. Neither let any
one raife fcandall upon this my writing of
Philofophy, but firft rather let him well
perufe and ponder every word; and then

it will appeare from whom I ſpeake , and whether I have this knowledge from the Devil, or from the experience of the pure light of nature.

Theo-

Theophraſtus Paracelſus
OF
Occult PHILOSOPHY.

CHAP. I.

Of Conſecrations.

Eeing God the greateſt of all good did in the beginning of the Creation of the World, plentifully and abundantly bleſs and ſanctifie all things which are therein ; both Places, Inſtruments, and all Creatures, that have their being upon the Earth; There is no need of other Bleſſings and Conſecrations; for he is Holineſs himſelf: wherefore all things that he ordained and made, are alſo conſecrated by and through him. Therefore no humane things do need any more or other Con-

ſecrafecrations; but may better, nay beft of all, be without them, efpecially fuch as fetting Croffes in the way. Croffes, Circles, Swords, Veftures, Candles or Lights, Waters, Oyls, Fire, Fumigations, Characters, Writings, Books, Pentacles, Seals of *Solomon*, Crowns, Scepters, Girdles, Rings, *&c.* and many other things of the like-kinde, which the Ceremonious Nigromancers do ufe againft the Phantaftick Spirits, as if they could not be compelled and bound by any other means; whereas Faith is the chief and principal Foundation againft them.

As often as the Ceremonial Nigromancers fay, that this is confecrated and bleffed, or that many Maffes are celebrated thereupon. Wherefore they all fay, that they are of power againft the devil and the malignant Spirits, who are terrified with fear and dread thereof, and flie there-from, *&c.* and dare not come neer it.

O you very arch-Fools, and ignorant men of no worth! even unworthy of the name of men, who do give Faith and credit to fuch monftrous and palpable lyes, when you fee notwithftanding examples thereof before your eyes; when fo much lightning falls upon the Temples, that it burns and deftroyes the Altars; which chiefly happens by the Tempefts raifed with Inchantments; alfo, when the Devil and the malignant Spirits are feen to raign about thefe places, and are heard by the Magitians what they fpeak. Therefore Negromancy with all its Ceremonies, is abfolute wickednefs, a Viper ufed amongft Juglers, a wicked work, which blindeth the eyes

of

of the spectators, deceiving them of their Money; but in truth is not to be esteemed worth a halfpenny, scarce a straw or rush : wherefore are not to be induced or made use of herein ; as *Judeus Solomon* in his book hath written, which the Nigromancers call, The Key of *Solomon.* For God would not have them to be used ; but hath given another thing instead thereof, to wit, Faith; which perfectly consecrateth all things. Neverthelefs, I would not have all Confecrations to be rejected, but onely thofe Ceremonies, which are aſſumed to be uſed againſt the phantaſtick and malignant Spirits. But I do not defire, that any thing ſhould be derogated from thoſe Magical Ceremonies and Operations, which are made for Phyſical uſes : neither, eſpecially the Confecrations in Matrimony, and in the Sacraments of Baptiſm, and the Lord's Supper, which are to be kept and obſerved by us in the higheſt eſteem and reverence alwayes, unto the laſt day. For at that time we are all perfectly confecrated, and ſanctified, and clarified with a heavenly body.

CHAP. II.

Of *Conjurations.*

BEfore we come to treat of Conjurations, whence they proceed , and what is the foundation of them ; It is firſt neceſſary to declare, who invented them, who uſed them, and what hath been brought to paſs by them ; and how more and more they came to be abuſed. Know therefore, that they had their original Spring and fountain from Babylon ; and there did mightily increaſe and flouriſh : afterwards it came into Ægypt, and from thence to the Iſraelites ; and laſt of all, to us Chriſtians. Amongſt the Nigromancers it is very familiar, and held in great eſteeme, ſo that in their rude and ignorant underſtandings, they all attribute more efficacy, power and vertue thereunto, then unto prayer and faith. This foundation, which is drawne onely from their opinions, is to be condemned, ſo that no man almoſt ought to remain therein ; but they all Juſtly deſerve to be puniſhed by the Magiſtrate who perſiſt therein. Although Conjurations may be able to effect ſome things in themſelves, neverthelefs they are not to be uſurped by any Magician or wiſe man, becauſe they are contrary even to God himſelf, and to his word and commandments, and alſo to the light of nature : For nothing of truth can
be

be forced or drawn from the Spirits thereby :
although they are fometimes forced to appeare
in their greateſt and Magnificent pompe, and
with terrible pride and haughtineſs, neverthelefs
they are not bound or overcome by this Conjuration ; for that can onely be done by faith a-
lone.

I fay, thofe kinde of Nigromancers who defire to perform and effeᶜt all things by their
Conjurations, fo as to compel, binde, afflict and
Torment the Spirits, forcing to do what they
will have them, are moſt like and fitly to be
compared to thieves and Robbers, that lurk in
woods and places to Rob and murder ; who can
kill and ſteale fo long, and fo far forth as God
ſhall permit them, but no longer : But when the
time and hour comes, that their villanies and
wickednefs ſhall be made manifeſt ; then not one
of the moſt fubtil and craftyeſt of them can ef-
cape : whereby it comes to pafs, that one for
Robbery receives his death, another is accufed,
and at laſt comes under the power of the hang-
man, who renders him a reward according to
the defert of his workes : No otherwife are we
to judge of fuch thieves who breake houſes and
ſteal fo long, till at laſt they periſh at the gallows.
So likewife doth the Nigromancer call and invo-
cate Spirits, conjure and afflict them with puniſh-
ments and Martyrdomes, fo long as he ſhall be
permitted by the Lord God; but not without the
curfe of God: and when the time and hour of his
puniſhment is come, then as the Proverbe is, he
receiveth his fruits: he erred in his Conjurations,

not

not drawing his Circle as he ought, out of the will and power of the Spirits, which they often fay unto him : To wit, thou haft erred in Conjuring, or thou haft not rightly drawn the Circle, thou haft not Chaftifed and prepared thy felf enough ; or that thy Seale and Pentacles are falfe : wherefore thou receiveft this punifhment : fo thy debts are paid thee in ready money , a long time referved for thee ; and which long fince thou oughteft to have had : fo he defervedly receiveth his reward from the Spirits, who leave fome notable eminent marke remaining upon him ; or mayme him in fome limbe or member, if not quite breake his necke : and by this he becomes his own executioner.

Therefore let thefe Ceremonious Nigromancers take heed and looke what they do; let them fet this chapter as a looking-Glafs before them, left by their own frivolous and wicked operation they themfelves become the fervants of the Spirits, and fuffer them to rule over them, and be their own executioners : Which being done, the Spirits will not fuffer themfelves any longer to be forced or compelled by thefe fervants ; neither will they do what they will, but now the fervants fhall be forced to yeeld obedience to the Spirits, who are become their Lords. The hang-man alfo doth the like, he hearkneth not to him that is to be fcourged, neither will he fhew any mercy or favor at the prayer of him that is condemned ; but he executeth the command of his Mafter, and what appertains unto his office.

Even

Even so also the Malignant Spirits are the hang-men and executioners of God, who can execute nothing without the commission of their Magistrate, that is, of the divine Majesty.

I say therefore that all Conjurations are against God, and are contrary to his word, the divine law, and the light of nature; which are prohibited to be used not onely to Spirits alone, but also such as are directed to herbs, stones and such-like, and especially those which are made against men; it becometh not us to act like the Heathens, who when they were not able to use men after their own wills, and could not force and compel them, they did Conjure them (as by many examples it is found in the Scriptures) so that they were forced and compelled to execute and act such things as were contrary to their wills and nature. Woe therefore to such wicked Knaves, and to all them whosoever imitate them: how great wickedness do they commit? And what grievous Plagues will come to them at the last, and what fearful and horrible accusations shall they heare the Devil make against them before the wrath of God? If afterwards it were lawful for them to signifie to such kinde of men, their misery which they endure, they who do such things, many thousands of them would be brought to repentance.

Chap.

CHAP. III.

Of Characters.

WE are not to give credit allo, neither to Characters nor Words; for the Poets and Negromancers do allo much exercife themfelves in them, and do fill their Conjuring-Books full of them, which they raife out of their own imaginations, meerly and rafhly, without any Foundation, and do feign them againft all Truth; whenas many thoufands of them are not worth a nut-fhell. But in the mean time I will be filent in their Characters, which they draw in Paper & Parchment, which are ufelefsly blotted with fuch trifles. It was a cuftome amongft thofe kinde of men, which amongft fome is hardly left to this day, That by impofing thefe Characters upon thefe men, they drew them to admiration of themfelves with thefe Characters, and fpeaking fuch words as are wonderful to me, and which were never heard of; yet they fay, they are found out and devifed by themfelves. Wherefore it is chiefly neceffary to have perfect knowledge, to difcern thefe Letter, Words and Characters.

There are many fuch-kinde of words found amongft them, which have no affinity at all with the Idioms of the Latine, Greek, or Hebrew Tongues, neither with any other; which cannot poffibly be interpreted by any man, nor rendred
into

into any other Tongue. Therefore I speak not without cause, and say, That we are not to credit all Letters, Characters or Words, but to keep to those onely which are true, and have been often proved, and taken out of the Foundation of Truth.

That we may come to these, and declare what Words or Characters are juft and true; we shall onely in the firft place detect and unfold two: although there may be found many other, yet neverthelefs, thefe are moft efpecially and principally to be accounted and efteemed of, before all other Characters, Pentacles, and Seals: note the delineation of them, which is thus:

Two Triangular Figures, cutting one another thorow with a crofs, are fo painted or engraven, that they do include and divide themfelves into feven fpaces within, and do make fix corners outwardly, wherein are written fix wonderful Letters of the great Name of God; to wit, *A-donay*, according to their true order. This is one of thofe Characters whereof we have fpoken.

There is another which excelleth the former in power and virtue, and this hath three Hooks cutting one another through by a crofs, and are fo delineated, that by their mutual interfection they include fix fpaces, and outwardly five angles, wherein are written five fyllables of the fupream name of God; to wit, *Tetragrammaton*, alfo according to their true order.

I would have put down the Figures themfelves; but becaufe you may happily finde them in many other

other places and Books, I have the rather omit
ted them.

By theſe two Characters ſome of the *Iſraelites*
and Nigromancers of *Judea*, obtained many
things; and they are now eſteemed of great price
amongſt very many, and held as great ſecrets:
for they are of ſo great virtue and power, that
whatſoever is poſſible to be done by Characters
and Words, the ſame may be effected by them
or one of them. I would gladly know, where
and in what place in all the Books of the Nigromancers may be found any other, wherein there
is made the like againſt the malignant Spirits,
Devils, & Inchantments of the Magitians, by all
the deceits and devices of theSorcerers.For they
do deliver him that is already inchanted either
in his minde or underſtanding, ſo that he is forced
or compelled to act any thing againſt his own
natural will or nature; or if he ſuffer any loſs or
hurt in his body, by the adminiſtration of theſe,
made in their juſt and due time and hour, and
being taken in his mouth with a Wafer, Pan-
cake,or ſuch-like thing, in four and twenty hours
he ſhall be free from the Inchantment.

There are alſo many other thing which are
helpful in ſuch caſes; as thoſe which ſhall be by
me laid down hereafter, when I come to ſpeak of
Tempeſts, and the Seaſons.

Briefly, theſe Characters are of ſo great force
and power, that if the Nigromancers did but
know and believe their power and and virtue,
they would forthwith reject and caſt away all
other things, even all their other Characters,
Words,

Words, Names, Signs, Figures, Pentacles, confecrated Seals of *Solomon*, Crowns, Scepters, Rings, Girdles, and fuch-like Ceremonies whatfoever, and wherein hitherto they have repofed any hope, thinking by them to fecure themfelves from their dangerous experiments and operations, when they would invoke, conjure, or think to compel and force the Spirits. Truely thofe which we have fpoken of, are the true Pentacles to be had and ufed againft all unclean Spirits, which they do all fear, even they which wander in the Elements. Neverthelefs, Faith doth ftrengthen and confirm all thefe things.

But fome may carpingly object, although undefervingly, and fay, That I break the third Commandment of God, of the firft Table of *Mofes*, wherein it is forbidden of the Lord God, for any one to take his name in vain. But who amongft any wife men, can be able to fay, That I have done this: or, that I have herein offended God ? whenas I ufe not this for that purpofe, nor after the fame manner, as the Nigromancers and Inchanters ; but onely for the extream neceffity and help of men, and in thofe difeafes and infirmities wherein no Medicines, no *Aurum potabile*, nor quinteffence of Gold, neither Antimony, nor no fuch fecret can help them, although they are of very great virtue and efficacy.

It becometh a Phyfitian to know the original caufe of all difeafes, that he may know which proceeds from evil meat or drink, as from Apples, Herbs, and other fruits of the Earth : and it
is ex-

is expedient for him to know the ſecrets of Herbs and Roots, *&c.* whereby the diſeaſe may be cured.   But if it happen under the cauſe of Minerals, ſuch diſeaſes are to be expelled by the ſecrets of thoſe Metals ; which the ſecrets of Herbs and Roots do not admit of, and have not power to do.

In like manner , if diſeaſes do proceed from the influences of Heaven , neither of the ſecrets aforeſaid, are able to profit any thing in the cure thereof, but it muſt be expelled by Aſtronomy and the heavenly influences, as it is written of *Parſicaria.*

Laſtly, if any diſeaſe or grief happen or be inflicted upon any man in a ſupernatural manner, by Inchantment or ſome Magical Sorceries, none of thoſe three remedies aforeſpoken of, will help them ; but there muſt be a Magical remedy whereby it may be expelled, as we have before delivered.

Many men who have in this kinde been made miſerable through inchantments, have alſo hitherto been forſaken and caſt off by the Ignorant Phyſitians ; becauſe theſe things hitherto were hidden unto them: And if they chance to be told them of others, they will anſwer, that if they ſhould uſe them, they ſhould act againſt God, and take his name in vain ; and that this which I have done hath no truth in it. But if I ſhould uſe theſe things to the hurt or prejudice of man, I ſhould Blaſpheme againſt God ; or if I ſhould Conjure any Spirits, man , herbe, roote or ſtone, &c. by his name, it might then juſtly
be

be ſaid that I did take his name in vain, and of-
fend God; but not before. Let the Divines themſelves alſo, and the Sophiſters ſpeake what they liſt
to theſe things, the thing which I ſpeake will not
be found contrary to the truth, although herein
their opinions may be very contrary unto me :
they will call me Inchanter, Nigromancer, and
a contemner of the Commandments of God,
which Calumnies and reproches I do not at all
care for : for it will be moſt certainly made manifeſt, that their exceptions againſt me, will appeare no otherwiſe then thoſe of the *Jews* and
Phariſees who carped againſt Chriſt, becauſe he
healed the ſicke on the Sabbath day : For they
ſaid unto him, that Chriſt had broke the Sabbath
and the commandment of God : the like they
did with *David* when he was forced and oppreſ-
ſed, and did eat the ſhew-bread ; But amongſt
theſe fault-finders and ſlanderers, how or what
ſhall be done that will pleaſe them all ? But the
Ignorant will not ceaſe to talke until the beaſts
or ſtones can teach them, which we muſt expect
will be a long time, and then they will hold
their peace.

CHAP. IV.

Of Spiritual viſions, appearing in dreames.

THere is a twofold kinde of viſions that do
appeare in dreames, that is to ſay, natural
E   and

and ſupernatural ; but various kindes of apparitions and viſions there are, which do appeare in
ſleepe and dreames, of which in this place it is
unneceſſary to make any mention, becauſe they
do moſt uſually happen, either by reaſon of ſor-
rowfulneſs, or ſome trouble and perturbation of
the minde, uncleanneſs of the blood, Cogitations, that is, operations of the minde and underſtanding, and occupations thereof about multiplicity of buſineſs and dealings that men are im-
ployed and converſant in ; as gameſters, of the
dice and chards, of great gain or loſs ; Souldiers
do dreame of warlike affaires, as of their gunnes,
pieces of Ordnance, Powder, Armes, and all
manner of weapons and inſtruments of war ; of
victory or overthrowes : the Sons of Bacchus,
and great drinkers, of good wine and great cups,
which they ſeeme to ſwallow ; and of ſuch other
things filling the belly : Pyrates dream of
their ſpoyles and preyes, and what gain they
have met with : Robbers, of Manſlaughters ;
theeves, of theft ; and fornicators, of their
whores. All theſe phantaſies and viſions the
Spirit of the night produceth and bringeth unto
them, whereby he playeth with them in the
night, and deludeth and tempteth them : Such
things are kindled in the blood, (*alias*) the underſtanding, and begetteth ſuch a fire, which cannot eaſily be extinguiſhed, which for the moſt
part may be ſeen in the venereous family.

Many wonderful Arts and Sciences alſo have
ſeemed to be made appeare to Artiſts in their
dreams ; the reaſon whereof hath been, becauſe
they

they have always had an ardent affection to thofe
Arts: fo powerful an imagination thereof, hath
for the moft part followed the fame, that they
have fuppofed in their dreames, that fome Phi-
lofopher hath taught them thefe Arts :this oftentimes happeneth,but the greateft part perifheth
in oblivion : fome rifing early in the morning,fay,
This night a wonderful dreame appeared to me,
even as that Mercury, or this or that Philofo-
pher corporally appeared unto me in a dreame,
who taught me this or that Art ; but it is fallen
out of my memory, fo that I cannot remember
any more thereof. To whom any fuch thing hath
happened, he ought not to go forth out of his
chamber, nor fpeak with any man,but to remain
alone and faft,untill he call to remembrance that
which he had forgotten. And thus much is fuf-
ficient to be fpoken concerning natural dreams,
and vifions appearing in the night in dreames of
what belongeth thereunto : But for the conclu-
fion of fuch kinde of vifions, one thing is
yet to be declared;thatamongft all thofe dreams
that do rejoyce our Spirits, grieve us, or caufe
forrow, commonly that which is the contrary
cometh to pafs: wherefore fuch like kinde of vifions are not alwayes to be credited.

But the other dreames which are fupernatu-
ral, are moft certain Ambaffadors, and true Le-
gats & meffengers fent unto us from God,which
are nothing elfe but Angels and Good Spirits,
who fometimes do appeare to us in our greateft
neceffities : Even as it happened to the three
wife men when they had come a great Journey

o ſeeke the young infant ; after they had found him, they would have returned to *Herod* , to tell him where the child was , and how they found him : but the Angel of the Lord appeared unto them in a dreame, ſaying , *Do not return to him, but return into your own Country another way.* For God knew the falſe heart of *Herod* , from which he ſpoke, wherefore he would not ſuffer his will to be performed. The like dreame happened to *Joſeph* and *Jacob,* when he would go into Ægypt : the ſame in like manner happened to *A-nanias* , *Cornelius,* and many others ; all whoſe dreams are ſupernatural: ſuch dreams do ſomtimes alſo happen to men in our times, but they are nothing eſteemed, yet neverthelefs they are not fallacious. We are likewiſe to know that theſe kinde of viſions may be obtained by us by prayer from our Lord God, in our greateſt neceſſities, ſo that our prayers be made with a ſincere heart , and with a true and undoubted faith, then he will at length ſend his Angel unto us, who will appeare unto us, and ſpiritually admoniſh, teach, and promiſe us.

Balaam was moſt expert in theſe kinde of viſions: for every night, as often as he would, he could obtain a viſion of this kinde: yet the Scripture hath given him an obſcure name, to wit, an Inchanter : it is not expedient to make any difference, for the Scripture obſerveth no difference herein, but calleth all them Inchanters who have experience and knowledge in the vertues of natural things ; nevertheleſs, great diſcretion is to be uſed in theſe things ; God would have

us

us to walke in simplicity, as the Apostles did, and not to search too deeply into such high, abstruse, and secret things above nature; that we fall not into the abuse thereof, and therewith hurt our neighbour : and so come into condemnation both of body and soule. They are not therefore all Inchanters which the Scripture calleth so : for then it would follow that those three wise men of the *East*, should be Arch-Inchanters; when as in all Arts, especially in such as were supernatural, they excelled all others before their time : therefore that the Scriptures do not call them Inchanters, but wise men ; what else can be gathered from them, but that they did in no wise abuse their Arts and occult wisdome? For Magicke is such an Art and science which demonstrateth and declareth the power and virtue thereof by faith: nevertheless Inchantments may spring from thence, to wit, when it is used abusively ; and before, it cannot be called an Inchantment.

But that I may speake more largely of visions in dreams; it is to be known, that some have been so spiritually lifted up to God in a dream, that they have seen his glory and the joy of the elect, and the punishment of the damned; which they could never afterwards forget, but have carryed the same in their hearts and mindes until the end of their life ; It is possible, I say, for us to see all these things in a spiritual manner: when we seeke for and implore the mercy of God, with a true faith and prayer, we may behold all the Mysteryes of God very well, as *Esaias* & *John* : These kinde

of

of viſions are certain and true; to which more
faith is to be given, then to all the precepts in Nigromancy by looking-Glaſſes, Chriſtals , Beryls,
nailes of the fingers, ſtones, waters, and the like;
for all theſe are falſe and fallacious: and although
ſuch Spirits do ſometime ſpeake in ſuch appear-
ances, and anſwer, and do aſſert the ſame with
an hundred Oaths, with erection of the fingers;
yet we are not alway to give faith or credit unto them, unleſs perchance it be done out of the
ſpecial command of God : otherwiſe they cannot
poſſibly ſpeake truth of all viſions, which we have
ſpoken of; thoſe Propheſies do come from a true
original, which do agree with all the Prophets.
From whence had the Prophets their wiſdome
and knowledge, and from whence were thoſe
Myſteries of God revealed unto them, by which
they had thoſe Spiritual and ſupernatural viſions
in dreams? It is neceſſary therefore, in the firſt
place, to the finde out the true foundation thereof, and to lay the ſame upon the right ſtone,
which is the word of God and his promiſes ; and
to pray daily unto God ; whereby it ſhall come
to paſs that he will give us all things which he
hath promiſed in his word.

   There is alſo another viſion belonging to
dreams, which we may take from them that are
dead ; and do appear ſpiritually unto us in
dreams, although they have been dead fifty or
an hundred years: this is very much to be taken
into conſideration : for many have undertaken
to treat thereof, which for their too much prolixity, (which we endeavour to avoid) we will
paſs

paſs them by, reſerving them to their place:
Neverthelefs this I will declare, (*viz.*) Where
it happeneth that one of theſe Ghoſts do appeare, it is moſt neceſſary diligently to note and
marke what he ſheweth unto us, what he ſpeaketh with us about, or doth ſpiritually Negotiate ;
and not always to account thereof as fables: For
if it were poſſible for a man to retaine the ſame
reaſon ſleeping, which he hath waking, that he
could aske and enquire of ſuch a Spirit, he
ſhould know the truth from him, about all his
deſires whatſoever : But it's not needful to
ſpeake any more largely in this place concerning
this thing.

Of Perſons and Spirits wandring under the Earth.

UNder the Earth do wander half-men, which
poſſeſs all temporal things, which they
want or are delighted with ; they are Vulgarly
called *Gnomi*, or Inhabiters of the Mountains:
but by their proper name, they are called *Sylphes*
or *Pigmies*: They are not Spirits, as others are,
but are compared unto them, for the Similitude
of their Arts and Induſtry, which are common to
them with the Spirits : they have fleſh and blood
as men, which no real Spirit hath: as Chriſt ſpoke
unto his Diſciples, when he came amongſt them,
when the doores were ſhut, and they were af-
fraid, ſaying, *Feele me, and touch me, for a Spirit*

hath

hath not fleſh and blood nor bones, as I have: By
this he himſelf hath taught us, that a Spirit hath
no true body that can be touched ; nor bones,
nor fleſh, nor blood, but exiſteth in its own
eſſence of winde or Aire. But of this we have
briefly ſpoken enough ; But to return to the
earthly *Pigmies* or halfe-men, we are to know
that theſe are not to be reputed Spirits, but like
to Spirits ; but if they are or ſhall be called
Spirits, they ought to be called earthly Spirits,
becauſe they have their Chaos and habitation under the earth, and not in the winde and Aire,
as the other Spirits have.

Many terrene earthly Spirits are found , ſeen,
and heard to be in ſuch places , wherein great
treaſures, and mighty ſtore of wealth and Riches
are hid ; and alſo under thoſe Mountains, where
there is plenty of Gold and Silver ; with which
things they are delighted, and do take the care
and cuſtody thereof, and not willingly do they
part from it.

Such as digge Metals have the beſt knowledge
of theſe Spirits, for they are moſt troubled with
them, and do vexe them , and much perſecute
them with blowes and ſtripes : ſomtimes alſo
they do afford benefits unto them, admoniſhing
them, and warning them of death : as when they
are heard once, twice, thrice or oftener to Knock
and ſtrike in the ſame place, it ſignifies the death
of him that diggeth or laboureth in that place ;
either he is buryed up by the fall of the Mountain, or dyeth by ſome ſuch occaſion : this is certainly experienced by them that do digge in
Mines.   Theſe

These Spirits are worst against those who do not appear to be Devils, and chiefly against those which they hate: but between these Spirits and the Devil, there is a great difference; because he dyeth not, but these perish after they have lived a long life, otherwise they might be called Spirits for this reason:but that which hath flesh and blood, is obnoxious to death, and ought once to die. There is another thing which we shall more largely declare from the common proverb, whereby it is reported that the Devil aboundeth in Riches, and possesseth much wealth, money, gold, and silver; and to have all treasures hidden in the earth under his power, and to give out of them what he will, to them that make any Covenant with him. And from hence that common saying tooke its beginning, that the Devil for this very cause giveth not onely Riches plentifully, and every thing that he desireth, gold or silver to any one that prescribeth himself unto him,& giveth up himself solely to be his,so as to renounce and forget his Creator.But I say that all these things are lyes and fained fables, without any foundation er ground; which ought to be rejected of every discreet and wise man:For the devil is the poorest of all creatures, so that there is no creature so miserable & poore, above or under the earth,or in all the other Elements. Neither hath he any money,nor Riches, nor any power over them;how then can he give to this or that person,thar which he possesseth not ? But he is infinitely skilful and cunning in Arts; and hath power to give and to teach them to those he
favor-

favoreth, and that he can wreſt away and delude with his deceit: he hath no money, neither gold nor ſilver can he give to any one; neither doth he ever take or require any bonds or obligations from men ſealed with their blood, or any other compaǆ or Covenant. But there are other Spirits which do ſuch things, ſuch as are the *Sylphes*, or *Pygmies*, which although they are perſons that are little by nature, yet they can appear to men as they will, great, or little; faire, deformed; rich or poore: they are not defeǆive nor wanting of knowledge in all kinde of Arts that are or can be found out in all the light of nature; but they have them, and contain the knowledge of them all within themſelves: they have enough of gold and ſilver, and the mines of all Metals under their power and cuſtody. In old times many of them have been found and heard amongſt men, but now they ceaſe; but no man hitherto hath known, or could give a reaſon of their ſevering and ſeparation, ſeeing they have alwayes been eſteemed to be Immortal creatures; becauſe no man could certainly be able to know or finde out their death, or could conſider any cauſe of their abſence: neither could any man for a long time be able to know what they now are, or whence they proceeded, or whither they wander, or what gift or office they have. Many do ſuppoſe that where they bring any benefits or good to men, that they are Angels, or good and familiar Spirits, ſent to thoſe men from God, and are afterwards by him taken from them, by reaſon of the greatneſs of their ſins: for oftentimes

times they bring to men very many good offices
and benefits, and do undertake and fuftaine
many hard labours for them.

Others believe that they will not be feen by
us, becaufe that when a man feeth them, he cry-
eth out ; fo that they vanifh away, and will not
appear any more.

Many that do fee or hear thefe Spirits, fuppofe
that they are the Spirits and foules of men that
have come to an evil death, fo that they have either defperately drowned or hanged themfelves,
or killed themfelves fome other wayes ; and de-
parting from God their Saviour, have given
themfelves to the devil : and for that caufe, do
wander about, and are referved by the devil unto
the day of the laft Judgement.

There have been fome who have fuppofed
that they are vaine Phantafies, and that they have
fore-fhown and prefaged much good fortune
to thofe places wherein they have been feen or
heard ; which many times alfo hath fo happened
and come to pafs : but for the moft part, faith effecteth it ; for of their own nature, they do not
bring any fortune, unlefs God compelleth them
or our faith. And on the contrary, they are not
able to caufe any misfortune, unlefs it be by the
permiffion of God.

And many do thinke that they are the Inchantments of the Magicians.

There are others who having feen and heard
them about treafures, have judged that they are
the Spirits of men, who have hid treafures in that
place, and ought to remain there until the the
Laft

Laſt Judgement, or untill their cuſtody thereof is found out ; and this opinion they receive from the words of Chriſt, where he ſaith, Where your treaſure is, there will your hearts be alſo. Bnt I do not ſee any reaſon why they ſhould underſtand the heart for the Spirit , but that there is much difference between them ; wherefore I ſay that all the Judgements which are ſpoken of before, are but falſe opinions, when as theſe are to be underſtood to be halfe-men, that bear rule and wander in the four Elements;and in the firſt and priſtine times of nature,they have been taken and worſhipped in ſtead of God : Theſe are they of whom God Almighty admoniſheth us in that Commandment of the firſt Table, ſaying , that we ſhall not have any other Gods but him , neither in the waters (where the *Nymphs* are underſtood) nor under the Earth , (by which he meaneth *Sylphes* or *Pygmies*) For the Lord our God is a Jealous God , and for ſuch an offence puniſheth the ſins of the Fathers upon the Children unto the third and fourth generation.

The Mountain of *Venus* in *Italy* , was much poſſeſſed with theſe Spirits for *Venus* her ſelf was a *Nymph*, and that Mountain was by a compariſon as her Kingdome and *Paradice :* But ſhe is dead, whereby her Kingdome ceaſeth to be : but where or in what place is there any mention heard to be made of them , as in former time, when *Danhanſerus* , and many others entred in unto them ? Neither did they Invent theſe fables : they were of ſuch a nature and condition, that they loved all men that loved them ;
and

and hated them that hated them:wherefore they
gave Arts and Riches in abundance, to them
who prescribed and bound themselves to them;
and they know both our minds and thoughts,
whereby it comes to pass, that they are easily
moved by us to come to us. I do not say this,
that I would give this Counsel to any one, but
that the true ground and foundation thereof
might be known, and the true difference which
is between the devil and these *Semi - homines.*
The devil hath not any body, unless he take any
thing to himself from the four Elements; for he
hath neither flesh nor blood: he remaineth per-
petual, not subject to any infirmities or a finite
death; wherefore he dieth not, but the *Pygmies*
do: nevertheless they are both subject to a natural and everlasting death, and are both de-
prived of everlasting life: wherefore whosoever
giveth or subscribeth himself unto them, the same
event happeneth unto him as to them: Let every
one therefore have a special care unto himself,
and consider well what he doth, before he subscribeth himself; for he suddenly doth that
whereby he shall alwayes be compelled to be
obedient unto them, and to fulfill all their com-
mands; And if he shall chance to be disobedi-
ent unto them, or anger them, they very much
impaire, or totally destroy and take away his life:
there have been found many examples of this
kinde, to wit, sometimes men have been found
dead, their neckes turned about, or otherwise
miserably handled: where any such thing hath
happened, it hath hitherto commonly been said,
that

that the Devil hath done this for this caufe, either that the man hath not kept his promife and compact with him, or that the time which he covenanted and fubfcribed himfelf unto him for, is expired; and that now he receiveth his laft reward. But thefe opinions do not proceed from the fountaine of truth : for the office of the Devil containeth no fuch thing in his power, but rather he fuggefteth unto men, evil thoughts and Cogitations, whereby he draweth them away from obeying the will and commandments of God; by which means he maketh them to be the greateft finners, and to forget and deny God their Creator : and afterwards draweth them into defpaire, fo that they cannot any more be able to pray unto God : wherefore the Elementary Spirits are moft like unto the devil, and oftentimes they are executioners of the wrath and vengeance of God; neverthelefs they do oftentimes alfo admonifh and warne us, and do watch over us and defend us from many dangers, and fometimes do deliver fome from prifon, and afford to men many other helps.

Wherefore fuch men as are burdened and overwhelmed with grief and forrowful Imaginations, are not to be left alone, but ought to be entertained with various and pleafant difcourfe, which may delight their mindes, and expel their forrow: The Devils likewife are in thefe cafes not idle; but as bufie as thofe terrene Spirits, & do eafily tempt fuch kinde of men. From hence it comes to pafs, that fome people, efpecially women in child-bed, have been fo oppreffed in the night in
their

their sleepe, that they have thought themselves
to be as it were strangled, neither could they
possibly cry out, or call any helpe, but in the
Morning have reported that they were Ridden
by a hag: And they are still accounted to be
witches, or Inchanters that do this; whereas
their bodies cannot possibly enter into the
chambers, where the doores and Windowes are
shut; but the *Sylphes* and *Nymphes* easily can.

O thou of little faith! as doubtful as *Peter*,
who suffereft thy self to be toffed with every
winde, and art easily drowned: thou thy self art
the cause hereof, by reason of thy little, dubious,
and weake faith; also thy evil thoughts do draw
thee unto this: Thou hast also in thy self a secret Magnes that attracteth every like. This is
the Celestial Load-stone above all others, which
attracteth Iron and steel, above the Quinteffence
and starry Magnes, which maketh the dejected
and hidden Iron to appear: for the Celestial Magnes is of such power and virtue, that from the
distance of a hundred thousand miles, even from
any place whatsoever, from the four Elements,
he attracteth the Iron to himself, when he passeth
into his own exaltation. But this we shall
make more largely to appear, in two excellent
examples following.

Of the Imagination, and how the ſame cometh into it's exaltation.

WHat powerful operation the Imagination hath, and how the ſame cometh to its hight and exaltation, may be ſeen by an example taken from experience in the time of peſtilence, where-in the Imagination poyſoneth more then any infected Aire ; and againſt which, no Antidote, neither of Mithridate nor Treacle, nor any ſuch preſervative, can exhibit any helpe ; unleſs that ſuch an Imagination do paſs away and be forgot-ten, nothing elſe will helpe. So quick and ſwift a Runner and Meſſenger is the Imagination, that it doth not onely fly out of one houſe into another, out of one ſtreete into another, but alſo moſt ſwiftly paſſeth from one City and Country into another ; ſo that by the Imagination onely of one perſon , the Peſtilence may come into ſome whole City or Country , and kill many thouſands of men : as may be underſtood by this example. Put caſe there were two brethren dearly loving one another, and one of them lives in *France* and the other travels into *Italy,* who is taken away by the Peſtilence in the middle way, and newes ſhould be brought to the bro-ther living in *France,* that his brother in *Italy* was dead of the Plague ; at which he being af-frighted, it pierceth through his Skin , into his Imagination, ſo that he cannot forget it ; and it is
kindled

kindled in him, and this fire doth so long rever-
berate and worke, as it may be seen in the tryal of Gold and Silver, which do send forth their
flowers so long, until they shine bright again;
which is not before they are perfectly cleare, and
separated from the other impure Metals: After
the same manner also the Imagination striketh
backe, and worketh it self unto the highest degree, after there will be a relucency thereof,
now it is received in a vessel in the man, as the
sperme of a man is received in the Matrix of
the woman, whereby the conception of the woman immediately follows. So doth the Pestilence
go from one to another, so long till it spread o-
ver a whole City or Country: It is good therefore to keep far off; not because of any corrupt
or infected Aire, for it infects not the Aire, (as
some Ignorant people say) but that they may
not see or heare the operations of the Pestilence,
which may infect their mindes. But those people to whom any such newes is reported as be-
foresaid, ought not to be left alone, neither
must they be suffered to muse silently with themselves, whereby the Imagination may labour in
their mindes ; but they are to be comforted,
and the Imagination is to be expelled from their
mindes, by exciting them to mirth and joy:
Neither let any think that I speak this as a fable.
as though it should seem to be a light business ;
neither is the remedy so easie for opprest Imaginations; for the Imagination is as it were pitch,
which easily cleaveth and sticketh, and soone
taketh fire, which being kindled, is not so easily

                                                    extin-

extinguiſhed : wherefore the onely remedy to
reſiſt the Peſtilence in ſuch men, is to quench
and expel the force of the Imagination. This is
one example wherein the power and operation
of the Imagination is declared, with the exhala-
tions thereof.

But now to ſpeake of another example, know,
that the Imagination doth not onely operate on
men in time of Peſtilence, and to deprive many
of their lives, but alſo in war : how many have
periſhed in war with the feare of the ſhot ? the
cauſe of whoſe death hath been onely their Imagination which they have had unto their death :
That is, they have been ſo greatly overwhelmed
with feare, and ſo terrified at every ſhot, that
they have thought no otherwiſe but that they
ſhould be wounded with every dart : ſuch men
are far oftner ſlaine then thoſe that are bold,
who go couragiouſly and without feare againſt
their enemies ; they feare no ſhot or wound,
but have a firm faith and hope of Victory beyond the other Souldiers ; ſuch are ſtout and
true Souldiers : how many Towers, Caſtles, Ci-
tyes and Countryes have ſuch warred againſt,
and overcome and Vanquiſhed the people thereof ? But the other that are fearful, whether they
be great or little, Noble or Ignoble, Knights,
Earls, or others, do ſcarce deſerve a halfe-peny
to go againſt an enemy, much leſs any wages.
Wherefore it becometh him that deſireth to be
an old Souldier, or to gain Knight-hood or any
honour in war, to fix and faſten his minde and
Imagination firmly upon ſome moſt excellent

ſtout

ſtout Head and leader of an Army, ſuch as *Julius Cæſar*,and many amongſt the *Romans* have been ; and by ſo doing,if he know how to uſe this Imagination well, and be of a firm and conſtant minde, and as he if would attain to and accompliſh all the heroick noble acts of ſuch a man; he ſhall not onely attain to be an old Souldier, but ſhall accompliſh his deſires in attaining to the like honours.

This hath ſuddenly happened to many who have followed the proceſs of their Imagination, ſo that they have attained to great honour and Riches.

Object. *But ſome may Object, that fortune, ſtrength and induſtry hath helped them, and promoted ſuch men; alſo , that ſome have worne herbs, rootes and ſtones,* &c. *by reaſon of the virtue whereof, they could not be overcome nor wounded.*

Anſw. I ſay that all theſe things are conſorts and helpers with the Imagination, which is the chiefe and general ruler over all others ; although I grant that there are many ſuch things, which do preſerve in the greateſt neceſſity againſt all enemies and their Armes, ſo that he that wears them,could not be wounded; whereof I ſhall make no mention in this place,but reſerve it to another. Nevertheleſs faith is the exaltation and confirmation of all thoſe things:for without faith theſe things and all ſuch like are vayne and void of ſtrength.

Of

Of treaſure and Riches hid under the Earth.

WE ſhall declare ſomthing concerning Treaſures hid under the Earth ; and ſhew ſome
meanes whereby they are known and gotten.
And alſo what things, ſomtimes evil, and wonderful, do happen about them.

The firſt thing to be treated of, ſhall be the
ſignes whereby they are known, that it may be
certainly made manifeſt, and not out of meere
opinion onely.

Note that it cometh to paſs, where ſuch places
are, that there do appear many Phantaſmes, and
ſomtimes immoderate ſtrange noiſes are heard ,
wherewith they that go out in the night are
ſtrucke with terror and feare ; ſo that ſomtimes
they are caſt into a cold ſweate, and their haire
of their head ſtands upright, which for the moſt
part happens on the Sabbath night. Alſo if any
lights do appear and ſeem to fall about thoſe
places, and there their light is extinguiſhed and
goeth out ; and ſomtimes there ſeeme to be
great flaſhes of wind in their houſe whoſe the
treaſure is, and where it is hid ; and there are
ſeene many viſions and ſtrange Phantaſies : and
many ſtrange Rumors and noiſes are there
heard. Where ſuch things happen, they are
heard and do ſhew themſelves moſt commonly
about the middle time of the night : And the
cauſe of theſe noiſes and ſights are , commonly
that

that there is treasure hid, in or about that place, neither is there any other reason thereof to be given. Neverthelefs many who have not underftood thefe things, have had many various opinions hereof.

Some have thought that thefe Phantafies have been caufed by the devil, or by fome Inchantment ; or by fome in that houfe who have fome worke or famliarity with the Devil, or who have given or bound themfelves to the devil, or have made fome promife unto him, whereby it comes to pafs that that wicked and malignant accufer caufeth thefe things to be feene and heard, that they might expect the expiration of their dayes, which he doth fo much defire fhould be fulfilled.

Others do believe, that fome have been fecretly died and buryed there ; others do thinke that fome wicked man hath died in that place, whofe Spirit hath been forced to wander thereabouts : and there have been other various and fundry opinions.

But all thefe Judgements are vaine and falfe, except onely thofe who conclude that the occafion of the noifes are, that there is treafure hid about that place; or that fometimes when the devil hath been driven out of fom body that he hath poffeffed , he hath been permitted to ftay about that place: but where thofe noifes are, it is a great Teftimony that there is treafure hid there.

There are two kinds of treafures hid;fome that may be found, and fome that cannot be gotten;

the

the difference whereof is this: such is eafie to be found, which containeth the Metals of Gold and filver, and are fuch kinde as we make, and have onely been ufed and handled amongft men : that kinde of treafure is not eafie to be found, which is Gold and filver, that is made, coyned, and hid by the *Nymphes* and *Sylphes*; which kinde of Gold and filver doth fomtimes come to be found and ufed amongft men, and is by the *Nymphes* fuddenly again buryed in the earth, and afterwards cannot eafily be found and gotten again.

Thefe things are moft worthy our knowledge, efpecially the fignes before fpoken of are moft diligently to be noted ; becaufe there are Magical Rods, which are deceitful, and are too eafily inclinable to bend to any money that is let fall or loft.

There are other vifions alfo which appeare in looking-glaffes, Chriftals, and fuch like things, which Nigromancers that dig treafures do ufe : but they are all falfe and deceitful ; wherefore there is little credit to be given unto them.

We come now to fpeake of the manner of digging for treafure, how a time may be taken that we may have a happy progrefs in the digging, which is as followeth. Firft, under an influence of the *Moone* or *Saturn*, and when the *Moone* tranfits *Taurus*, *Capricorne* or *Virgo*, is a good time to begin to feeke. or dig after treafure. Neither need you ufe any other Ceremonies, nor to draw any Circles, or to ufe any Inchantments whatfoever ; onely thofe that dig muft be of a cheereful minde, free and aliena-
ted

ted from any evil thoughts or cogitations, and not to be moved, nor feare any phantasies, visions, or Imaginations of the Spirits: although they should corporally appeare, yet they are onely visions. Therefore those that dig ought to discourse, sing, and be cheereful, and not to be affrighted at any thing, but to have a good courage: And by no meanes soever let them keepe silence, as some perfidious Negromancers have taught.

Now when they come neere to the place where the Treasure is, that it is almost detected, and do heare many noises; and strange visions and horible sights are seene, which oftentimes happens to be: It sheweth that the *Pygmies* and *Sylphes* are there, who do envy that men should have those treasures: and will not willingly part from them, especially if it be their own, or such as they brought thither. Such treasures are to be left, if the keepers thereof consent not. And although they may be gotten and taken away as a Robbery from those keepers, yet these keepers have an Art whereby they can change these treasures, in this way gained, into a vile and base matter, as into earth, clay, dung, and such-like things, (as I have seene by examples:) wherefore when any such transmutations happen, we are not therefore to despaire in our mindes, although we find nothing like either Gold or silver, neither would any one suppose any such thing to be there. We ought therefore to fly to the holy Scripture, which saith thus, God shall judge the world by fire; and in the Psalmes thus,

Gold

Gold and filver are tryed in the fire, and are found pure and cleane : wherefore in any fuch tranfmutations, the fire ought to be the judge ; the proceeding in the tryal thereof, ought to be after the fame manner , as the refining and feparating of minerals and Metals ; And by this meanes, it will be forced of neceffity to return to the fame effence which it had before.

There is another thing remarkeable in thefe kindes of tranfmutations ; for fomtimes the diggers are deluded, and there are found oftentimes pots of earth, full of brafs, ridiculous things and matter, as bones, egge-fhells, pieces of wood, and fuch things, which have been buryed there many years before. And they that have found the fame , have fuppofed it to be the true treafure, Gold or Silver, and to have been changed by the evil Spirits ; which is falfe. For treafure found fuddenly and unfought for, cannot be changed by the Spirits, but remaineth in the fame fubftance which it had before. Therefore thefe things are not to be accounted a tranfmutation, but rather a vexation: for fomtime thefe vexers of men do bury fuch things, that they which feeke after the treafure might labour in vaine: Therefore fuch things are not to be regarded, which are of no worth, and may eafily be known by the lightnefs of their weight ; But if they be of a heavy and ponderous body, like to a Mineral or Mineral fand, there may an experiment thereof be made by fire.

That we may omit nothing that may conduce hereunto, we will adde alfo this objeftion.
Some

Some may aske, How comes it to pafs that Treafure is fomtime eafily found which is not fought
after ? The caufe whereof we may fuppofe to be
this. Thofe Spirits which are the keepers of
treafures, do beft know the mindes, thoughts,
and cogitations of men : therefore becaufe
they know, that men have not any thoughts or
will to dig or feeke after any treafures in fuch
a place, they give no diligence to keepe the
fame, neither do they fufpe&t it; whereby it
comes to pafs, that it is eafily taken from them.
It happeneth to them, as it doth to thofe men
who fuddenly get fome prey from their enemies,
they not thinking of them, whereby the are eafily overcome, or fpoiled by them. There are
two caufes chiefly why treafures are fo greedily
fought after by men. The firft is the Covetouf-
nefs of them who thirft after riches; & the other,
that thofe places where the treafures are,might be
afterwards made habitable,fecure, fafe, and quiet
from being infefted or molefted with fuch Spirits. For there are at this day many ancient
houfes and Caftles which are inhabitable, by
reafon of thefe kinde of Spirits: and the chiefe
caufe thereof is, that there are great treafures
hid about thefe places. In thofe places where
fuch things happen, it is chiefly neceffary that
great care be taken in the digging thereabout;
not fo much for the money and treafure, as that
the place may again be made quiet and habitable.
When any one goeth about this worke with
diligent digging, one of thefe things commonly happens ; either the treafure is found, or
carried

carried deeper in the earth, or removed by the keepers to ſome other place ; as viſions in pure Chriſtals have often ſhewn, and as they have told the diggers : I now ſee many *Pygmies*, take the treaſure quite away. Credit ought to be given hereunto, and the digging to ceaſe.

It is further to be known, by how much the greater noiſes are heard about the place, and fights and viſions ſeen, by ſo much greater the treaſure is to be judged to be, and neerer to the ſuperficies of the earth.

Chap. VIII.

Of thoſe that are poſſeſſed of malignant Spirits, and of the Devil.

AFter what manner men are poſſeſſed and overcome by the Devil, the Apoſtle *Peter* largely writeth and declareth unto us : But that the words of his admonition may be underſtood according to the true ſence thereof, a little ex-poſition is needful : For the Apoſtle briefly and ſummarily comprehendeth the whole matter in two words, to wit, faſting and prayer : Theſe ſeem to be very little and light things at the firſt ſight ; neverthelefs they are of very great Moment, and ſignifie very many things, if they be conſidered rightly and attentively : When therefore the Apoſtle *Peter* doth ſo earneſtly ad-moniſh us, ſaying, Be ye ſober and watch : for
your

your enemy the Devil goeth about as a raging
Lion, seeking whom he may devoure; Afterwards
he concludeth, that by faith we may be able to
resist the Devil ; therefore *Peter* would have us
to understand his first word of Sobriety, so, as
if he should say, Beware of all kinde of glut-
tony and drunkennefs.

For drunkennefs is the fountain and original
of all evils and vices, which are acted and com-
pleated by drunkards through the perfwasions of
the Devil : wherefore obferve a mean in meat
and drinke, left your hearts be troubled and burdened therewith ; for the Devil is alway prefent, although invisible; he is a Spirit, and understandeth all Arts, and can be in what place he
will, throughout the Circuit of the whole earth :
he is the author and Actor of all evil and wickednefs which is done by men in the whole earth;
he is as watchful over mankinde, as a Cat is over a
moufe : wherefore he seduceth you unawares,
when you have filled your felves with wine ; and
then filleth up all vices in you : he then compaf-
feth you about with his fnares and bonds, as the
hang - man doth evil-doers and malefactors, untill he hath killed them ; so alfo doth he with
thofe that are drunke ; besieging them with
fnares and Temptations, untill he either hath
destroyed their bodyes, or brought them into
despair.

Take heed to your felves therefore, Oh you Epi-
cures and drunkards, and alfo Souldiers, who are
always filled with wine night and day. Therefore
a fouldier that fo overchargeth himfelf with meat
or

or drinke, ought to be accounted brutiſh as ſwine, ſeeing both of them are Ignorant and uncertain of the time of their death, or how ſoone they may be ſlaine.

This is the meaning of the firſt word of St. *Peter* of Sobernefs:now we come to underſtand what he meaneth by watching.

By watching *Peter* ſeemeth to underſtand, as if he ſhould ſay, Walke in uprightneſs and juſtice; be of good courage, not faint-hearted; caſt away all evil thoughts and cogitations, and all Phantaſies of the Devil, that ſuch Imaginations may not have any place with you; For hereby many have been overwhelmed and beſieged by the devil, the reaſon whereof hath been their own wicked and evil thoughts and Imaginations. Therefore relinquiſh and caſt them all away, and have God always before your eyes; pray unto him, and let him be onely in your thoughts; make your ſelves like unto him and his children, and then he will ſend you his holy Spirit, who will guard you, rule you, and declare the wonderful workes of his mercy by you, as he hath done by *Paul* and all the other Apoſtles, who have been all after this manner preſerved by his holy Spirit; follow them therefore, and exclude and caſt away the Devil and all evil cogitations, and wicked thoughts, wherewith we may alſo ſeduce and deceive our ſelves, and thereby attract and draw the devil into us, and be corporally beſieged and poſſeſſed by him, and ſo come into deſperation, that we may deſtroy our own lives; even as did *Judas, Achitophel,* and many others.   Thus

Thus much of watching,& the interpretation thereof,which *Peter* would have to be underſtood thereby. For by watching he doth not mean abſtinence from the bed and ſleep, as the *Carthuſians* and other *Monaſteries* do teach and obſerve; for God created and ordained reſt and ſleepe, and firſt ſuffered it to enter into *Adam*. Wherefore every one ought to ſleepe in due ſeaſon, as much as his nature requireth, &c.

Laſtly, note how *Peter* concludeth and confirmeth his word from God, ſaying, Let us reſiſt the devil by faith ; as if he ſhould ſay, Do not in any wiſe ſticke or ſtumble at the word of God, or doubt of his mercy; do you not burden your conſcience , nor trouble your hearts ; do not perſwade your ſelves thatGod regardeth you not, or that he is forgetful of you ; or that he accounteth you unworthy of his mercy, ſo that you ought not to come unto him, becauſe you have acted againſt his Divine will, or have broken his commandments, and committed many ſins : But rather,firmly believe his word, that Chriſt would not the death of a ſinner, but rather that he ſhould be converted, and live : Alſo, that he came into the world becauſe of our ſins, that he might take them from us upon himſelf ; which alſo he hath done : there are many ſuch comfortable words to be found in the Holy Scriptures,which ought to be propoſed to ſuch perſons as are weake in their faith, for their comfort and conſolation : After this manner a man reſiſteth an evil conſcience and the Devil, ſo that he is freed from them, and not tempted any more. *Of*

CHAP. IX.

Of the manner of delivering them that are poſſeſt
by evil Spirits, and the great abuſe which hither-
to hath been committed by many, in ſuch kinde
of buſineſs.

NOw to come to ſpeake of the driving away
of evil Spirits; it is to be known, that very
few ſince the times of Chriſt and his Apoſtles
have rightly been driven away. For they knew
not how to uſe any other meanes but Ceremo-
nyes and Conjurations, wherewith they en-
deavored to expel the malignant Spirits and the
devil ; whereas this is altogether a falſe foundation, and by no meanes to be followed or imi-
tated. Although ſometimes ſome have been
delivered by this way, and the devil hath been
driven from them ; neverthelefs it hath not
been done, neither can it be done without loſs :
Like as if a Prince would vanquiſh ſome Country
or City, with the Sword, this he could not poſſibly do without ſome apparent damage and loſs
to that place. A common proverb hereby cometh to minde, which ſaith, That he that cannot
get good words from good men, ſhall much leſs
wreſt them from evil men, although they be
compelled by force: the more evil is to be feared,
as by examples is too often ſeen to come to paſs.
Therefore that opinionated power is to be re-
                                              linquiſhed

linquifhed which is ufed in Ceremonies and
Conjurations. But you ought to expell wicked
Spirits as Chrift and his Apoftles did, and no o-
ther way : But if you do otherwife, you undertake great Labours againft the Devil: for certainly the Devil is forced through great difficulty to
go out of men, and feeketh all iniquities and wicked occafions to ftay, and retain them in his
power. But when he feeth that he can no longer
ftay, and remain in the poffeffed, but is forced to
go out, then he requireth power and licence to
enter into fome other man, or beaft, or into
fome other place : which if he be permitted,
there followeth a greater lofs thereupon.

Therefore there is no other place to be permitted or affigned unto him, but hell, from
whence he cometh, and which God hath ordained for him, and caft him into; that it may not happen, as we have an example (as we faithfully believe) when Chrift permitted the devil which he
caft out of the man, to enter into the herd of
fwine, which no fooner had the devil entred into them, but they were drowned in the Sea.
Therefore they are in no wife to be permitted to
enter into any other men, left fuddenly after
they deprive them of their lives, as they did
thefe fwine : Neither are they to be permitted
to go into any Rivers, lakes, or ponds ; which
if it fhould be done, they will drown many
men therein, and draw them into the deepe under thofe waters; and will deride them as a fool
doth his mafter with his fingers ; and therewith
the devils are more delighted then before: neither
ought

ought they to have any power given them, or to
their deſires to go into any houſe or Caſtle; for
they will perpetually poſſeſs it, and will ſo reigne
there, that no body will any more be able to
dwell or inhabit in that place, but they will alway be inhabitable, as many both houſes and
Caſtles are in many Countries, which are left de-
ſolate for this very cauſe; many whereof I could
name in this place, but I paſs them by, to avoyd
prolixity: let Satan therefore aske what he will,
where, or to what place he would go, nothing
elſe ought to be granted to him, then to return
into hell, which God ordained for him, and thruſt
him into: from whence he came into the man,
and into which he ought to enter when he goeth
out of the man, &c.

    Alſo if the devil ſhall cauſe the man to ſpeake
many vaine trifles, we ought not to anſwer thereunto, or to ſpeake much with him: But if any
one will ſpeake with him, let him ſay, I command thee, Oh thou unclean Spirit, by the word,
power and virtue whereby thou wert caſt out by
Chriſt & his Apoſtles, that thou go out of this man,
&c. He is no other way to be conjured; neither
are theſe words to be taken for a Conjuration,
but for an anſwer, by which alone he is not caſt
out: but this is firſt to be done, to wit, to watch
and pray; for Chriſt ſaith, This kinde is onely
to be caſt out by faſting and prayer with faith.

    Wherefore it is chiefly neceſſary to induce
and force ſuch as are thus poſſeſt, to prayer;
though it be very difficult to be done, becauſe the
devil ſo Ruleth their tongues, that he ſuffereth
them

them not to pray : Therefore there muſt be
prayers made before them ; and if they will not
pray with and after thoſe that are praying, they
muſt be more ſharply dealt withall ; That is to
ſay, the poſſeſſed muſt be faſt bound both his
hands and feete, and afterwards let ſome o-
ther man lie acroſs over them , and ſhew himſelf to be very angry with them, and ſeverely
compel them to prayer: but he ought to pray before them, and to exhort them to pray after him
the ſame words. By this meanes ſuch people
may be induced to pray, when they cannot be
brought to it by any other meanes ; which ought
to be continued day by day,and the devil will go
out of them and leave them. This ſhall ſuffice
to have ſpoken concerning the caſting out of un-
cleane and evil Spirits, becauſe I am reſtrained
to uſe brevity in other places.

Chap. X.

Of *Tempeſts*

THat we may now come to ſpeak of the original of Tempeſts, & how they may be expelled away ; Alſo how and by what meanes any
one may preſerve himſelf and his from Thunder,
lightning and haile: We ſhall declare in the firſt
place , that all Tempeſts do proceed from the
four Capital windes, *viz.* the *Eaſt, South, Weſt,*
and *North* : Then from the Centre of both,
G that

that is to ſay, of the Aire and Firmament , there
are no tempeſts can ariſe ; But from the four
Fountaines before ſpoken of, which comes chiefly to be conſidered.

Wherefore he that deſires to preſerve his
goods, Houſe, Lands, garden, field, meadow, and
ſuch things from all manner of thunder, haile
and Tempeſt ;   he ought firſt to know theſe
things,whereby he may alſo know how to aſſimi-
late inferiours to Superiours. We will therefore
in this place briefly declare the original of all
Tempeſts.

The original of tempeſts is certainly nothing
elſe,but the appearance of Spirits ; and lightning
or corruſcation preceding , is the preſence of
them : whereby it may be certainly known,whe-
ther thoſe tempeſts will paſs away with or
without danger; and that after this manner is to
be underſtood ; to wit, as a ſtranger will not enter into any ones houſe, unleſs firſt he ſpeake, ſo
theſe Spirits do not appeare unto us without
ſpeaking firſt.But their voice is thunder,which as
we ſee immediately follows every flaſh of lightning. Alſo if a ſtranger ſhould ſuddenly fly into
the houſe of another, where he is not known ;
it ſeems to ſignifie no good,but evil rather; either
he himſelf is proſecuted by others,or elſe brings
ſome damage to them. So likewiſe are we to
underſtand of the lightning of heaven ; the more
quick it comes, the more dangerous it is,for commonly ſome Thunder-bolt followes. It is therefore very neceſſary to know how every one may
defend and ſave himſelf herefrom,that he fall not
                                          into

into fome place that he would not, or receive
fome other hurt : the Ringing of Bells do availe
nothing in thefe cafes ; although I do not reject
them, efpecially in fuch tempefts as are caufed
by Magicians inchantments, by reafon of the
Spirits by them raifed in the Aire. For the Spirits do love filence and quietnefs, whereby it
comes to pafs that great noifes, as the founds of
bells and Trumpets, do partly diminifh and difperfe tempefts by them ftirred up : But in
Thunders and haile they do no good, as the
Monks and Sacrificers have to their lofs too often
found. And for this caufe they ufed ceremonies, wherewith they feduced the Vulgar and
common people, perfwading them that befprink-
ling places with holy water (as they call it) preferved them fafe from Thunder and haile ; likewife by burning holy candles, or fome palme,
or other herb by them fanctified, or with the per-
fume of Frankincenfe, or Myrrhe of thefe facrifi-
cers they were preferved fecure.

O thou fool, and unwife facrificer and Monk,
who art hitherto Ignorant of thefe things ; and
underftandeft them not, in this place thou mayft
be taught the contrary ;how that Malignant Spirits
are not driven away with fweet perfumes, but
are mightily delighted therwith, and do run more
freely & fwiftly to them, then to ftinking fmells ;
whether they be good Spirits or evil. But if in
ftead of Frankincenfe and Myrrhe, you had taught
to have made a fumigation of *Affa Fetida*, you
might therewith drive away both good and evil
Spirits : For the good odour of Frankincenfe

and

and Myrrh is nothing elſe but the ſacrifice of the Spirits, wherewith we attract and draw them unto us. But of this we have ſpoken enough.

Now to return to that which we intended to write of, and firſt, how any place may be preſerved from Thunder and haile : note therefore, that to place a preſervative in the centre of a houſe, garden, or field, &c. availeth not at all ; but at the four Angles, *Eaſt, Weſt, South,* and *North* ; then the place ſhall be ſecured: as a building ſet upon four Pillars is more ſtrong and firme then that which is founded onely upon one , which is ſet in the middle of the centre, or ſome other place : this is more eaſily overthrown by the winde or Spirits. Now the materials which belong to this preſervative, and of which theſe four pillars are made, note that they conſiſt of ſimple bodies, every one whereof is ſufficient, and hath ſtrength and virtue in it ſelf for the effects before ſpoken of : As Mugwort, St *John's* wort, Perewincle, Celandine, Rue, Devils bit, and many ſuch herbs and roots, and eſpecially if they be gathered and taken in the right influence.

There are alſo other things of far greater ſtrength and vertue ; as Coral, Azoth ; and one of the Characters before ſpoken of being drawn in a certain table, or ingraven : In theſe three things is a great ſecret againſt all Inchantments and workes of witches and the Devil himſelf. In which preſervatives we may truſt in our greateſt neceſſities.

Of

CHAP. XI.

Of the great abuse of the ᴄMagicke Art by them that use it for Negromancy and Witch-craft.

THe Magicke Art in it self, is the most secret and occult science of all supernatual things in the world : That those things which are impossible to be searched out by humane reasons, by this Art, to wit, Magick, it may be found out and known : wherefore it is the most occult and secret wisedom; and reasoning against it, is nothing else but extream folly. It were therefore very necessary that the Divines would learn to know something of this Art, and be experienced in Magick what it is ; and not so unworthily, without any ground at all, to call it Witchcraft. The Magical science were very profitable for them to know, seeing they will undertake to be the Masters and teachers of the holy Scriptures, and perswade themselves to be so : Not that I would have them use the Magical Art, or operate any thing by it ; but to be expert therein, and to know the virtues and effects thereof, for the high and great mysterious secrets which are hidden in the holy Scriptures, delivered by the Apostles, Prophets, and Christ himself; and which we by our humane reason cannot understand nor search out.

What Divine that is Ignorant of Magicke,

can

can caſt out the Devil, drive away or binde a
Spirit, or that can call one unto him, and command him to come? or that which is far leſs, can
he heale the ſick, or adminiſter any other help to
him by his faith alone? I wil be ſilent of his remo-
ving a mountain into the Sea. There followeth
then that faith whereof Chriſt ſpeaketh, of which
they underſtand neither much nor little: Nevertheleſs they make a great ſhew and profeſſion
thereof with their mouthes, and do teach and
ſpeake much thereof; but themſelves know not
how to make proofe thereof, or to give any
ſigne thereof, by their faith, whereby it may be
ſaid that they underſtand this faith, and to make
uſe of it in the proofe thereof. But if any one
ſhould come, who by his faith and Magicke
ſhould perform a good ſigne, you having not the
reaſon of knowing whether it be good or evil,
will forthwith call him a Negromancer and
Witch, becauſe he hath done ſomething above
your reaſon and humane wiſdom; when you your
ſelves cannot tell how to diſcerne a Negromancer or Witch, from a Magician.

Magicke is therefore a moſt neceſſary and pure
Art; not defiled nor corrupted with any Ceremonies or Conjurations, as Nigromancy: For
in Magicke there is no uſe of Ceremonies, Conſecrations, Conjurations, Bleſſings or Curſes;
but of faith alone whereof Chriſt ſpeaks, ſaying,
that by it we ſhall be able to remove Mountains
and caſt them into the Sea; And to compel, looſe,
and binde all Spirits: This is the true foundation and Inſtrument of Magicke.

Truely

Truely therefore it is a thing chiefly neceſſary to looke into this ART, that it be not turned into ſuperſtition and abuſe, and to the deſtruction or damage of men ; and hereby it is made Nigromancy, and Witch-craft ; and at length, not undeſervedly, ſo called by all men, becauſe Witches and Sorcerers have violently intruded themſelves into the Magicke Art, like Swine broke into a delicate Garden. So is Magicke corrupted and made Nigromancy by theſe perfidious men ; wherefore it hath not undeſervedly been burnt in the fire with theſe Witches and Sorcerers. For theſe kinde of men are the moſt nocent and hurtful, and the worſt enemies to mankinde, that they have not worſe enemies in all the world, which proſecute them with a more deadly hatred : from a preſent publique enemy, and corporal perſecuter, who endeavoreth to invade us with the moſt cruel weapons, Guns, or Darts ; we may beware of ſuch a one, or take up Arms againſt him for our defence, with Brigandines or Darts, &c. or elſe a man may tarry in his houſe, and keep himſelf, ſuffering none to enter in but his Friends. But of theſe Witches and Sorcerers, no man can beware or defend himſelf, becauſe againſt this kind of Enemies of God and men, no Weapons, Coats of Mayl or Brigandines will help, no ſhutting of doors, or locks ; for they penetrate through all things, and all things are open unto them. And if any one were incloſed in Towers of Iron or Braſs, he would not thereby be ſecured from theſe enemies ; Although in their own proper

bodies

bodies they ſeldom bring hurt to any one, but raiſe up, and ſend Spirits unto them, by their corrupt Faith, and hurt them in ſome part of their bodies, although they are abſent from them an hundred miles diſtance; they either ſmite, wound, or kill them, although no outward and external wound can be ſeen appear: becauſe they cannot hurt the outward man, but only the internal ſpirit. Wherefore no Coats of Mayl can defend them, be they never ſo good; but they muſt put on other weapons and fortifications, to wit, the Armor of Faith: This is the true way, and then let him be clothed with a Linen garment, the wrong end turned upwards: and after that hath been often worn, thou ſhalt be more ſafely delivered, than if thou wert armed and girt with all manner of weapons.

Although there are many preſervatives which will keep and defend men from all theſe Faſcinations and Witchcrafts which are wrought by the ariſing of theſe evil Spirits, ſuch as are Coral, Azoth, and the like, which being uſed according to their due uſe and order, will well preſerve from theſe enormities before ſpoken of. For the prevention and preſervation from them is eaſie, but the cure is difficult; nevertheleſs it is poſſible: But in ſuch caſes, the proceeding thereunto muſt be magical and ſupernatural: From thence ſprung that ſaying which ſome uſe, That none can better help the bewitched, than them that hurt them: This is a true ſaying which cannot be contradicted: but they which uſe it, underſtand not the Cauſe of this thing, neither can they give any
reaſon

reaſon thereof, why Witches do beſt of all, moſt happily, readily, and ſurely help, and Cure the bewitched: Therefore of this thing you ſhall be here ſufficiently inſtructed.

Some Witches make and form Images in the form and likeneſs of ſome man which they propoſe to themſelves, and conceive in their own minds ; and do ſtick a nail in the ſole of his foot, and after this manner hurt the man , that he invifibly feeleth the pain of a nail in his foot, and is ſo tormented therewith, that he is not able to go, until the nail is pulled out of the foot of the Image ; which being drawn away, the man is healed: which no man knoweth better how to do, than he that fixed the nail in the Image; nor where it was fixed, or what the Cauſe of the Diſeaſe was.

It oftentimes alſo cometh to paſs, that after the ſame manner a nail is ſomtimes by theſe witches fixed in the teeth of the Image of the man, ſo that afterwards he cannot take any reſt in his teeth, unleſs the nail be taken away, or his teeth drawn out: In like manner are nails ſtruck into any other members of the Image by theſe arch-Sorcerers, and hereby they hurt men without making any impreſſion or ſigne thereof upon their skin.

Oftentimes alſo it ſo happeneth to men, that there ariſe Tumors in their heads or elſewhere about their bodies, which are like Puſhes ; or sky-colour ſpots, that appear ſuddenly and vex men in their bodies, as if they had been beaten with knotted Ropes : to whom any ſuch accident
hap-

happeneth without any viſible blow or bruiſe to be perceived; he will not judge any otherwiſe, but that he is ſmitten by theſe Images.

It is too often ſeen to fall out, that a man ſometimes loſeth an Eye ſuddenly, or is ſtruck quite blind; or deaf in one, or both Ears; dumb, or ſome imperfection in his ſpeech; crooked, lame, or dieth; all which accidents are wrought by Witches, through the divine permiſſion: All which are Magical acceptions and torments, and are made and completed by the Aſcendants.

In theſe Caſes the Phyſitians ought to take heed, and be adviſed, that when they perceive ſuch kinds of Diſeaſes to be ſupernatural, that then they do not judge them to be natural Diſeaſes, and ſo think to Cure them with their common Apothecaries Medicaments: For thereby they will reap nothing but diſgrace, which often happens to many of them: It is a croſs (ſay they) or affliction by God laid upon them, which no Phyſitian can help. Oh you Quackſalvers, it is not as you think, but indeed it is a chaſtiſement, by the permiſſion of God, wrought by Witches and evil men; wherefore the Phyſitian ought to conſider the Signs, whereby he may know, and judge of the Diſeaſe; and thereby may inform himſelf which way to effect the Cure thereof: And Medicines are to be uſed, and applied thereunto.

In the firſt place it is neceſſary that he ask the Patient, How, and in what manner the Diſeaſe took him, or happened unto him; what was
the

the original of the evil, Whether it were occa-
sioned by any fall, blow, thrust, bruise ; or if any
other natural Cause can be perceived ; or that
there be any Flux, or inward corruption of blood:
but if none of these signs appear, then let him a-
gain demand of the Patient, Whether he hath a-
ny body in suspition that is an enemy, or one not
wishing well to him, that might be a Witch? If
he answer that he hath some mistrust of any such,
then he shall judge that it hath happened to him
as is above declared. Therefore it is most necef-
sary for the Physitian to understand rightly after
what manner he is to deal with the Patient, if he
desire to be perfect in this art. But the Ancients
have not written at all any thing concerning this
kinde of Cure, neither *Galen* nor *Avicenna*, nor
any other ; we shall therefore lay down the
manner of the Cure in Order, which follows.

They who are bewitched, cannot be Cured
any better, than by hurting again the same place
afflicted ; that is, by making (through Faith and
imagination) such a like member as is hurt, or
else a whole Image out of Wax, which he shall
either anoint or binde up with Plaisters , where
the Tumors, Signs, or Spots be, is a present help
for that person in whose name it shall be made ;
and the pain shall cease, *&c.* But if he be so bewitched, that he is in danger to lose an eye , his
hearing; or be impedited in the Generative fa-
culty of his privy Members, in his Speech, or
hath his Members made crooked or wreathed a-
wry ; then let there be made an Image of the
whole body of Wax, with a firm Faith, upon
which

which Image let the intent of your imagination be firmly fixed; and afterwards let the whole Image be conſumed with fire in due order. Make no wonder that people bewitched are thus eaſily Cured: neither be like the Sophiſters of the Academies, who ſcoff and deride at ſuch things; and ſay, That they are impoſſibilities, and againſt God and Nature, becauſe they are not taught in their Schools.

It follows then, ſince they are true, That a Phyſitian ought not to reſt only in that bare knowledge which their Schools teach, but to learn of old Women, Egyptians, and ſuch-like perſons; for they have greater experience in ſuch things, than all Academians.

We come to ſpeak alſo of the Dartings and Jaculations of all Witches, as the Inchanters and Witches do call them; when they afflict any man, that they inſert aſhes, hairs, feathers, briſtles of Hogs, fins of Fiſhes, and ſuch like things into the foot, or ſome part of the body, without any opening of the skin.

But how, or after what manner this is done, we ſhall not here ſpeak of; leſt if it be known to ſome, it may be by them made uſe of to do evil; wherefore we ſhall paſs it over, it being only neceſſary to write of the manner of the Cure, that the ſame likewiſe may be effected without opening of the skin, and ſuch griefs taken away. The way and uſe of the Ancients in ſuch kinde of Cures, is eſpecially to be avoided, who uſed to lance the part affected with Razors, about the centre thereof, and that very deep, where there
are

are no hairs, nor any thing elſe to be found ; and
by that way of proceeding, do afflict the Patients
with moſt intolerable torments, as if they were
racked in the hands of the hangman : for by
this kinde of Remedy, very few are Cured, but
many have thereby loſt their lives. Wherefore
this proceeding is quite to be left, and a better
to be choſen : which is : Let ſome quantity, the
whole, or half, much or little, of the like injaculated matter, which may be found and buried either in an Elder or Oak, and fixed with a wedge
towards the Eaſt ; which being done, there needs
not any greater labor, for then that which remains may be extracted from the body, and the
Cure will follow without uſing any other Remedy : But it will be otherwiſe, if the extracted
matter be not placed in a right place; whatſoever
it be, it cauſeth hurt, and diminiſheth not the injaculated matter. Wherefore it were to be
wiſhed, that it might be extracted from the body
of man, without labor or pain, without making
any inciſion, combuſtion, or opening thereof : It
is therefore eſpecially to be noted, that the ſame
ought to be done by the virtue of the Magnes,
(which attracteth all bewitched matter to it ſelf)
ſuch as is Oak-leaves, Celandine, Azoth, and
powder of Coral : which if any one of them be
by himſelf bound and faſtned about the Centre,
in 24 hours it will extract from the body all ſuch
matter, as by any ſuch means of Witchcraft is
injaculated therein.

I ſhall only add this one thing, which is a common ſaying, uſed by many to ſay, I am an enemy
to,

to, and hate fuch Witches and Sorcerers; wherefore I am fure they cannot hurt me : And this is firmly believed by fuch kinde of faithlefs and ignorant men, that thofe Witches and Sorcerers that they hate , can do them no hurt ; but only fuch as they love, and give fomthing to, &c. But this is falfe: for whofoever they are that are their enemies, do alfo give them thereby an occafion to ufe hatred and enmity towards them ; and from that Spring at laft arifes the Perfecution, according to the manner, power, and proprieties of the enemies. But if we would refift them that they cannot hurt us, we muft do it by Faith ; for that confirms and ftrengthens all things, raifeth up, and cafteth down, and performeth all things.

The end of Occult Philofophy , of Paracelfus.

P A-

PARACELSUS
Of the Mysteries of the Signes of the Zodiack :

Being the Magnetical and Sympathetical Cure of Diseases, as they are appropriated under the Twelve Signes ruling the parts of the Body.

The Prologue.

T is without doubt, that many will be much ravished with admiration, when they see these my Writings brought into the light, because of the admirable effects & vertues which are found in Metals, being first rightly and
duely

duly prepared with the hand and art: which among many people, are held and accounted to be superstitious and wicked operations, and against nature; that they are idolatrous operations, and that the help of the Devil is used to bring them to perfection. They say, How can it be possible, that Metals being engraven upon only with Characters, Letters and Words, should have any such power, unless they were prepared through the Craft and Assistance of the Devil? To these we Answer, I hear you give Credit to them, and do believe that they have power and virtue, being prepared by the help of the Devil, and do operate through him; And are you not able also to believe that God, who is the Creator of the whole Work of Nature, hath as much power in Heaven, and also that he giveth power and virtue to those operations in Metals, Herbs, Roots, Stones, and such like things? But in your judgment you seem to make the Devil more wise and powerful, than the only Omnipotent Lord God, who of his great Mercy, hath Created all Metals, Herbs, Roots, Stones, and all things whatsoever, that live, or move, in, or upon the Earth, Water and Air; and hath
endued

endued them with their feveral degrees of virtue, for the benefit and ufe of mankind: It is alfo moft certain, and approved by experience evidently, That the Changes and Mutations of time, have great and powerful ftrength and operation; and that chiefly in Metals, which are made in a certain determinate time, as it is manifeft to many, and very well known to us by fundry experiences. No man likewife can teach that Metals are dead fubftances, or do want life; feeing their oyls, falt, fulphur, and quinteffence are the greateft Prefervatives, and have the greateft ftrength and virtue to reftore and preferve the life of man, before all other Simples, as we fhall teach in all our Remedies affigned thereunto: Certainly if they had not life, how could they help Difeafes, and reftore the decayed Members of the Body, by putting life, and ftirring up corporal vegetation in them: as in Contractures, the Stone, Small-pox, Dropfie, Falling-ficknefs, Phrenzy, Gout, and feveral other Difeafes, which for brevities fake I omit to mention. Therefore I fay, That Metals, Stones, Roots, Herbs, and all other Fruits have life in them, though of divers kinds, according to their Creation and growth,

H and

and the due obſervation of the time con-
tingent thereunto.   For the times have
in them ſingular power and virtue ; which
manifeſtly appeareth, and may be proved
by ſundry Arguments, which we ſhall not
here produce, ſince they are ſo commonly
known.   For it is not our intent here to
treat of things that are ſo cleerly known ;
but of more weighty and undiſcerned ſecrets, which to ſence ſeem contrary.

Characters, Letters, and Signes, &c.
have ſeveral virtues and operations ;
wherewith alſo the nature of Metals, the
condition of Heaven, and the influence of
the Planets, with their operations, and the
ſignifications and proprieties of Characters, Signes, and Letters, and the obſervation of the times, do concur and agree
together. Who can object that theſe Signs
and Seals have not their virtue and operations, one for infirmities in the head, being
prepared in his time ; another for the
ſight ; another for gravel in the Reins and
Stone, &c. but every one is to be prepared in his own proper time, and helpeth
ſuch and ſuch infirmities, and no other ; as
drink is to be taken within the body, and
not otherwiſe : but all this is to be done
by means, by the help and aſſiſtance of the
                                        Father

Father of all Medicines, our Lord Jefus
Chrift, our only Savior.

But if any one fhall object, that Words
and Characters have no virtue; and fay as
well as others, That they are of no more
power than a bare Mark, or naked Crofs
or Signe; Alfo, that ὀπόχωνθξ, hath no
more power in the Greek tongue, than in
the German, but only fignifies the death
of a Serpent, or fome fuch thing : Let him
tell me, who believeth fuch things, from
whence it comes to pafs, That Serpents in
Helvetia, or *Suevia*, do underftand thefe
Greek words, *Ofil, ofija, ofil*; fince the
Greek tongue is not fo vulgar in thofe
Countries, that venemous worms fhould
underftand it, or in time learn it ? How
fhould they come to underftand them, or
in what Univerfitie have they learned
them, that as foon as ever they hear thefe
words, they will immediately ftop their
eares with their tayles, that they may not
hear them again ? For no fooner do they
hear thefe words, but immediately they
lie ftill, contrary to their natures, not hut-
ting, or offering to bite or caft any venome
at any man; and afterwards if they hear
any man to approach towards them, they
fuddenly fly into their holes. , If thou doft

fay

say that nature doth effect this, it is the same which I did expect thou shouldest answer: but if Nature worketh this upon a Serpent, why doth she not the same among all other Creatures ? But if you should say, That the noise of the mans voice effecteth it, and that thereby the Serpents are terrified and stupified ; or that it is done by any power in the man ; why then do they not in the same manner lie still when a man maketh a far greater noise, either crying out, or dischargeth a Gun, or the like ?

Characters and Seals have likewise in them wonderful virtue, which is not at all contrary to nature, nor superstitious : Also, if you say that words are of no effect, but as the bare voice of men ; I say on the contrary, if you write the same words in Parchment, or Paper, in a selected time, and put it upon a Serpent that is taken, in what manner you will, he will remain and lie still, as if you had spoken the same words.

Neither is it any wonder, that Medicines can help men not taken into the body, but only hanged about the neck as Seals : For it is common to the Bladder with Cantharides, That it turneth his Urine into

into Blood , that holdeth Cantharides clofe in his hand, the Bladder holding the Urine, and containing it that it cannot pafs out of the Body, the hand being held far from the Body.

Some Creatures do retain the fame vir-tue after they are dead, as I prove by the Bird called the *Kings Fifher*, whofe skin being taken off from his carcafe, and being dried, and hanged up upon a nail, will caft his feathers many years, and new ones will grow again; and that not only for one or two yeers, but many yeers one after ano-ther.

But if you further enquire, out of what Author or Writer I read of thefe virtues, or where I learned fuch experience; I an-fwer you Sophifters and Contemners of the Gifts of God, that very Nature her felf demonftrated before your eyes, doth far excel all the Authors and Writers of the world.   I pray tell me which of your Authors or Writers taught the Bear, when his fight is dimmed by reafon of the abun-dance and fuperfluity of his blood, to go to a ftall of Bees, which by their ftinging him, pierce his skin, and caufe an effufion of the fuperfluous blood ? ·What Phyfi-tian prefcribed the herb Dittany to be mecine for the Hart? or who taught the Serpent the virtue of Briony and Dragonwort? who taught the Dog to take Grafs for his Cordial and Purge? And who prefcribed the falt Sea-water to the Stork for a Clyfter? Did you teach this knowledge to them? or do not they teach you? The fame might I fpeak of infinite other Animals, that know naturally the Cure of their own Difeafes. What! Have the Bruit-beafts taught the Medicinal Art? If you fay, It's a Natural inftinct, and that Nature teacheth them, fo fay I too. If Nature hath infufed fo much reafon into Bruit-beafts, how much more fhould men learn thereby, who are made according to the Image of God, the Creator of all things; and are indued with reafon from God, to confider and contemplate fuch things?

Alfo to fay that things outwardly applied, and not fubftantially entring into the body, cannot Cure any Difeafes, is falfe: For the Sun, which giveth us light, warmth, fplendor, and infufeth life into all things, penetrateth into the moft occult and clofe Manfions of the Earth; and doth vivifie and quicken all things that lie under the earth, even to the centre thereof.

For

For who can deny that in Spring-time, especially, the Sun penetrateth into the most secret places of the earth, giving heat and warmth thereunto, when it shines only upon the upper part thereof? From whence the roots of all things therein receive juyce, strength, and life? and why therefore may not the splendor of Nature, and the influences of the Heavens, Stars, Planets, and other means which we use to extract out of Metals, Herbs, Stones, and such like things, give their virtue into the bodies of men, and penetrate into the inner and private members thereof? as into the Nervs, Veins, and other internal Defects lurking in the flesh and blood of men, and have been there a long time growing. Diseases, Infirmities, and Accidents, are divers; so likewise are the several Cures thereof to be opposed to them according to their qualities, in their peculiar dayes and times: Against which also, Metals do best of all help; being prepared and used in due time and means: As if I should undertake to Cure the Leprosie with Gold; what should hinder but that an Oyl made thereof may Cure it by Unction? Also, if I should anoint the Small Pox with Oyl of Mercury, do you

think

think I am able to Cure them with this
Mercury? without doubt; especially if I
observe a fitting time for this purpose,
without which last means, all anointings
are in vain, although the sick were bathed
in Oyl of Mercury : But in such Diseases
where the Mercurial medicines are not suf-
ficient, we ought then to use other remedies : which unless I should do, having a
due respect to the observation of time, not
only the Unctions, and all labor besides,
will be vain and fruitless, but they will
bring the Patient into a worse condition :
for it is most certain, that Diseases come to
men for the most part from the power and
influences of the Stars upon the bodies of
men, yet not so suddenly that the same can
presently be perceived, like a stripe, or the
Falling-sickness. But they do encrease in
process of time by little and little as it were
a distillation, as oyl causeth water to wax
fat by drops falling into it. A man may also perceive his own defects, by the shrinking or decaying of his Members, loss of
Appetite to meat and drink, pain, &c. according to the condition and property of
every Disease, the operations of the Stars,
and the accidents by the Air, prepared and
attracted upon us.

PARA-

PARACELSUS
Of the Myſteries of the Signes of the Zodiack :

Being the Magnetical and Sympathetical Cure of Diſeaſes, as they
are appropriated under the
Twelve Signes ruling the parts
of the Body.

CHAP. I.

Of the Common Griefs of the Head.

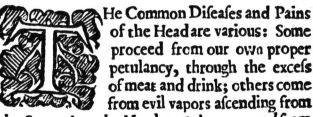He Common Diſeaſes and Pains
of the Head are various: Some
proceed from our own proper
petulancy, through the exceſs
of meat and drink; others come
from evil vapors aſcending from
the Stomach to the Head, and they proceed from
several

ſeveral Cauſes, which in this place we intend
not to treat of; but only of the more grievous
Diſeaſes of the Head, which follow.

CHAP. II.

Of the Falling-Evil.

THe firſt thing to be taken notice of in this
Diſeaſe, is the ſigns of the Falling; whether they happen at certain equal times, months,
dayes, and hours, and how often; or whether
they be unequal, happening at divers times; and
whether a little before they fall, the Patients do
uſe to ſhake and ſtagger a little, or whether they
fall to the ground ſuddenly, and unawares: which
being perceived, if they fall at certain times and
hours, then the Diſeaſe doth not take them ſo
ſuddenly; neither do they preſently fall. But if
it come at unequal times and hours, the contrary will be ſeen to happen; to wit, the falling
comes upon them unawares. The firſt kind, to
wit, when there is a little ſhaking and ſtaggering
before the fall, is mortal: But if they perceive
the fall before it come, the Diſeaſe is accounted
not to be ſo dangerous, but more Curable; which
proceedeth not from Nature, as the firſt; nor is
not common therewith, wherfore it leſs weaken-
eth: The firſt brings Phrenſie, and Madneſs; but
the other is a falling Diſeaſe. The Cure of theſe,
is thus;

Firſt,

First, Consider in what day, and what hour he Fell the last time, and write it : then see what Planet rules that hour ; also the sign and degree of the Patient are to be known.

Then the yeers of the Patient are to be numbred, and his Sex, which also keep noted in writing ; then give this Medicine every day in the morning to drink ; which followes,

℞ of the Spirit of *Vitriol,* Quintessence of *Antimony,* each 5 drops. Quintessence of *Pearle,* 4 drops.

Give all these in the morning to the Patient to drink in a little draught of Rose-water , and let him fast four hours afterwards : Let him use this proceeding by the space of 29 dayes ; and in the mean time, prepare the *Lamen* following , made after this manner,

℞ of *pure Gold,* ʒ ſs. and when the *Moon* comes to the 12 degree of *Cancer,* then lignifie the *Gold* in an Earthen-pot , and then let it be poured out into pure clean water. Afterwards mark when there comes a Conjunction of two Planets in the Heavens, and at that time precisely melt again this *Gold,* and in the point of the Conjunction, poure in ʒ ſs. of the most perfect and fine ☽ , that there may be an equal mixture of the ☉ and ☽. When this matter is poured out, and cold, make it into a Plate, that it may be four fingers bredth on both sides; then cut it into the form of a *triangle,* as appears in this figure.

Heate

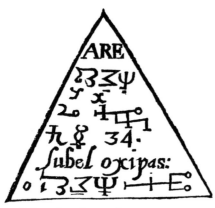

Heat this *La-men* very hot in the fire, and then let it reft until you find the *Moon* in the fame figne & degree that fhe was in at the time of the coming of the laft fit before; and in the fame hour, carve and ingrave thefe Signs and Characters, beginning with the Letters as they are fet uppermoft, in the *Lamen* of *Gold* and *Silver*. And you muft make hafte, that the Figures and Marks be all made and finifhed in the fame hour, or elfe all your labor is in vain. The figne of the Planet of the hour in which the Fit of the Difeafe fell, is firft to be engraven in the middle of the *Lamen*, as you may fee it is in this foregoing Figure, which was made for *James Seitz*, Bifhop of *Salisburgh*, now living; who fell in the hour of ☿ : Make the reft of the Signes as you fee in the Figure, only this excepted, that for a Woman, inftead thereof you fhall put this Cha-

racter: and under the other the Age of the Patient, as in the Figure you fhall fee 34, fo many yeers old was the faid *James Seitz*. Therefore the number of yeers is to be written to every Difeafe according to the Age of the Patient   The

The Figure being now prepared according to the directions; after a Fit cometh, command that his Hair be shaven off from the Crown of his Head, according to the Latitude of the *Lamen*: Then presently where he fell and lieth, with art and industry pour some of the Secret before prescribed into his mouth, and so hold him that it may descend into his Stomach; then forthwith apply the *Lamen* to the place shaven, so that the Sculpture may touch the naked flesh, and let it be bound on that it fall not off; which being done, let the Patient be carried to some place where he may quietly sleep. And after that Fall, without doubt he will never Fall more, although he hath had the Disease 30 yeers: But let him always wear the *Lamen* about his neck, and shave his Hair at every Months end, in the same place where they were first shaven.

CHAP. III.

Some other Figures to Preserve the Sight.

MAke thee a round *Lamen* of the best Lead in the hour of ♀, the ☽ being in the Signe ♈, and in the same hour; to wit, in the hour of ♀, engrave the Signes and Letters which you see written in the following Figure: Afterwards in the hour of ♄ make a *Copper Lamen* of the same Quantity and Form as the Leaden one; when ☽ is in the signe ♑, the Characters which you

you ſee in the Figure, are to be engraven. And then both Figures are to be kept and preſerved ſo long until ♀ comes into Conjunction wich ♄: and then in the point of the Conjunction both the Figures are to be conjoyned together ſo, that the Characters and Signes may mutually touch one another; then cloſe them faſt with Wax, that they receive no moiſture, and ſew them up in a piece of Silk, and hang it about the Neck of the Patient on the day and hour of ♀. This is the beſt Remedy to recover the Sight of the Eyes, and to preſerve the Eyes from Pain and Diſeaſes. It preſerveth the Sight in old Age, as perfect as it was in youth.

To Preſerve the Sight.

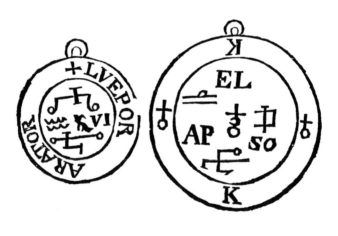

CHAP. IV.

Againſt Drineſs in the Brain, and other Diſeaſes in the Head.

TAKE of the following Metals, well re-fined:

Of *Gold*, ℥ ſs. Of *Silver*, ℥ ii. Of *Copper*, ℥ i. Of *Tynne*, ℥ iii.

Let them be all melted together in the point of the new Moon; then pour them out, and of that Maſs make a piece of Plate of what Latitude you will: After that theſe Metals have been melted together, they muſt not be put into the fire any more. When the Planet ♃ is in his own Houſe, to wit, in ♓, let theſe Characters and Signes be engraven in the inner-ſide of the Mo-ney, and in the back-ſide of the Money let thoſe words be written which you ſee in the follow-ing Figure, in the ſuperior part of the Circumfe-rence of the Money: then let there be made a Ring of *pure Gold*, and affixed thereunto when the Moon is declining, for it to be hanged by: it matters not in what day the Ring be made, ſo that it be done in the hour of ☉. This Money being thus prepared, let it be hanged about the Neck of the Patient in the point of the new Moon.

Moon. It is of wonderful operation againſt all Diſeaſes of the Head, and Brain.

For Diſeaſes of the Brain.

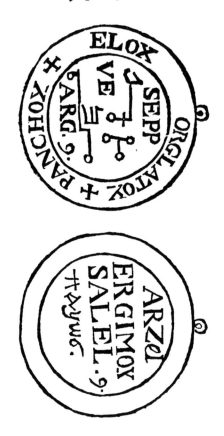

CHAP. V.

Againſt the Palſey, a moſt excellent Secret.

FOr the Conſolation of thoſe that are afflicted
with the Fits of the Palſey, to write a Remedy thereof, that not without cauſe, it may be
called my Archidox, ſeeing it excelleth all other
Cures : Although ſome Ancients have thought
(but falſely) that this Diſeaſe is incurable. Therefore if any one be in any manner taken with this
Diſeaſe, let him thus do,

Rx of *pure Gold*, ℥ ii. of *Lead*, ℥ ii.

Both theſe Metals ought to be moſt purely re-
fined. And firſt, when the Sun ſets, going under
the Earth, in the ſame hour (which you ſhall calculate according to the time of the year)melt the
Gold in a new Earthen melting-pot, made and
prepared for this purpoſe. Which being done,
immediately after the Sun is ſet, caſt the Lead into the Gold, and forthwith pour them out together, for the Lead will be diſſolved by the Gold
in a moment : Keep this Maſs. Afterwards when
☽ is in the 12 degree of the ſigne ♌, melt again
this matter of. ☉ and ♄, and it will appear like
Bell-metal; to which adde 3 drams of ♀: but let
it not be long in melting, but pour it out, and
keep it. Then when ☽ comes into the 12 degree

I   of

of m, melt this matter again, and caft into it one dram of ♃, & prefently pour it out; but caft it into a broad form, becaufe it admits not of any impreffion neither of the Hammer or Sciffers. Then keep it till ☉ enters into the figne ♈, which commonly happens every yeer on the 10 day of *March*: Then engrave the Characters with the Signes and Words on both fides as you fee them drawn in this Figure, and begin to engrave them in the hour of ☉, and finifh them before the end of that hour. It needs not be obferved what day the fame be done, only this, that ☉ be in ♈, as is abovefaid. The Money being thus prepared, is to be kept; And when the Palfey taketh any one, let the time, day, and

Againft the Palfey.

hour be diligently enquired of the beginning of the Difeafe; and the fame hour of that day, let the Signe be hanged about his Neck. This is a great Myftery: but in the mean time let the *Aurum Potabile* of our defcription be adminiftred to the Patient. CHAP.

CHAP. VI.

Against the Stone and Sand in the Reins.

THe Money against the Stone, consists of 4 Metals: to wit, of Gold, Silver, Tynne, and Lead : As followeth.

Rx of *Gold*, ℥ iii. of *Silver*, ℥ iii. of *Tynne*, ℥ i. of *Lead*, ℥ i. ſs.

Let all theſe Metals be melted together in a new Melting-pot for Gold, on *Saturday* at 1 o of the Clock before noon, ☽ increaſing ; which being melted, caſt in Saltpeter mixed with Tartar, for this cauſe only , to make them the more tractable, and eaſie to be molten and wrought upon. Afterwards, let them be poured out and caſt into the form of a *Lamen*, and let it be cut, and poliſhed, and filed in the hour of ♂ and day of ♀ ; but as yet, let nothing be engraven thereon. Alſo, the Ring is not to be forged, that it come not into the fire any more after the melting, but is to be formed with a File : wherefore the *Lamen* is to be poured out, and caſt the larger and broader, that the Ring and *Lamen* may be both one piece. And if it can be, let the *Lamen* be ſo poured out after the melting, that by the mixture of divers Metals, eſpecially of the Lead and Tynne, the brittle matter may evade ;

and

and the ſubſtance remain hard, that it may not
be wrought with the Hammer, nor cut with Sciſ-
ſers. This being done, then look for the *Moon* ;
and in the point of the *New Moon,* then begin
the Sculpture : and make haſte, that one ſide of
the *Lamen* may be finiſhed in that hour, which is
marked with the Letter *A.* Afterwards, let this
Money be ſafely kept until ſome day of ♃, when
☽ is in Aſpect with ſome good Planet, as ♃, ♀, or
☿ ; then let the Words and Characters be engraven on the other-ſide, marked with *B,* in the hour
of ☿, as you ſee them in the following Figure.
Then let the *Lamen* be hanged about the Neck
of the Patient that hath the Stone, when the
Moon is decreaſed, on the day and hour of ☽. The
Ring ought to be made of Iron, to which the *Lamen* is hanged. Let the Patient alſo drink Wine
every morning, wherein the ſaid Seal hath been
ſteeped all night, and afterwards hang it about
his Neck again. This doth wonderfully expel
the Stone, and Sand or Gravel out of the Reins ;
for which thing alſo Spirit of Roman *Vitriol* is
good to drink.

For the Stone in the Reins.

CHAP.

CHAP. VII.

Of the Members of Generation.

THe loſs of Strength and Virtue in the Members of Generation, is a certain Sympathy proceeding from groſs Fatneſs, which as a certain *Spaſma* impedites the power of the Members of that place. This happens by divers accidents; ſome whereof are natural, others are againſt nature, by Witchcraft. For the Remedy of the natural Paſſion, we uſe this remedy : Let theſe Words, with the Characters adjoyned, be written in new Parchment, which afterwards is to be bound about the nut of the yard.

A V G A L I R I O R σαλιχιαλοια וֹבֹיא

This Writing in Parchment ought to be renewed every day by the ſpace of 9 dayes, before Snn-riſing every morning, by binding it, or rowling it with the Writing backwards about the Prepure, and there let it remain night and day ; and as often as you renew the Parchment, or change it, let the old-one, which you take off, be burnt to aſhes, and let the Patient drink it in a draught of warm wine. This is a moſt excel-

I 3   lent

lent Remedy, to be had with the leaſt coſt. But
if any one deſires to be preſerved from theſe e-
vils, let him wear about his Neck a *Lamen* of Silver, with the ſame Words and Signs engraven
thereupon : Or if one make a *Lamen* of Gold,
and engrave the ſame Words and Characters
thereupon, it will be far better. But when it
happens that this Diſeaſe is brought upon
any one by Witchcraft, or ſome Diabolical Art,
wrought by the malice of wicked people; let the
Patient take a piece of a Horſe-ſhooe found in
the high-way, of which let there be made a Tri-
dent-Fork on the day of ♀, and hour of ♄, as
you ſee in this Figure following.

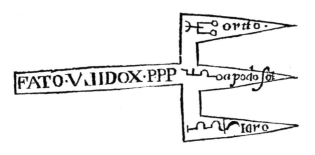

The Fork aforeſaid being made, let thoſe
Words with their Characters be engraven upon
the Three teeth, as you ſee in the Figure. And
upon the Handle thereof, thoſe Words and Signs
which you ſee in the Figure, on Sunday before
Sun-riſing : which being done, let the Fork be
faſtned in the ground under a running Stream of
Water, ſo deep, that the handle may not be ſeen,
and that it cannot be found : by this means, thou
ſhalt

ſhalt be delivered in 9 dayes; and the perſon that hath wrought this miſchief upon thee, ſhall get ſomthing himſelf in that place, from which he ſhall not ſo eaſily be delivered: So we ought to reſiſt Diabolicall Arts by Nature, as Chriſt by the holy Scripture propoſed to the Devil in the Wildernefs.

CHAP. VIII.

That a Horſe ſhall live Sound a long time.

SOme will think that I write Witchcraft, or ſome ſuch like things; which are far abſent from me. For this I certainly affirm, That I write nothing here, which is ſupernatural, and which is not wrought and effected by the power of nature and Celeſtial influences; and whereof, for the moſt part, we are not altogether ignorant. As this: Let a Sadler make a Bridle for a Horſe of a Lyons Skin, and upon the Reyns thereof let theſe Words and Characters following be written in their certain time. And you ſhall perceive this Horſe to live not like a Horſe, but like a Man; and longer, and his ſtrength not to be abated: So that you do not uſe him extraordinarily, contrary to his wonted cuſtome. Alſo, according as you apply thoſe Bridly-reins to him, he will live thirty or forty yeers, more or leſs, contrary to the common term of a Horſes life. The Bridle is thus to be prepared, that it ſerve

I 4   him

him for a Halter, without a Bit. The Leather-
Dreſſer ought to prepare this Skin in the hour
of ♃, that is, then to put it into his Pit; which
being ſo prepared, let the Sadler cut the Thongs
of it in the hour of ☉, and afterwards make it
into a Bridle when you will. To this Bridle is
to be affixed the *Lamens* following in the hour
of ☿ upon the Thong of the Head, made of
Tynne.

S. U. R. Q. L. R. E.

Upon the Thong,
going down from
the Fore-head to
the Noſe, let there
be affixed theſe which follow, made of Copper
in the hour of ☽.

♃ ♄ φ. λ. y. π. ω. S E L E.

The following *Lamens* ought to be made
of Silver, in the hour of ♃; And affixed to the
Bridle in the hour of ♃.

A. K. R. X. X. X. X. X.

Theſe which are
laſt, ought to be
made of Gold,
and affixed to
the Bridle in the
hour of ♂. 3. 9.

And apply this Bridle to the Horſe in the
hour of ♀, then you ſhall ſee with what power
Nature

Nature worketh in Words and Characters, where time is duly observed.

CHAP. IX.

An admirable Oyntment for Wounds.

SImpathy, or Compassion, hath a very great power to operate in humane things : As if you take Mofs that groweth upon a Scull, or Bone of a dead body that hath lain in the Air, to wit,

> Take of that *Mofs,* ℥ ii. of *Man's Greafe,* ℥ ii. of *Mummy,* and *Man's Blood,* each ℥ fs. *Linfeed Oyl,* ℨ ii. *Oyl* of *Rofes,* and *Bole-Armoniack,* each ℨ i.

Let them be all beat together in a Morter fo long, until they come to a moft pure and fubtil Oyntment ; then keep it in a Box. And when any wound happens, dip a ftick of wood in the blood, that it may be bloody; which being dryed, thruft it quite into the aforefaid Oyntment, and leave it therein ; afterwards binde up the wound with a new Linen Rowler, every morning wafhing it with the Patients own Urine ; and it fhall be healed, be it never fo great, without any Plaifter, or Pain. After this manner, you may Cure any one that is wounded, though he be ten miles diftant from you, if you have but his blood.

It

It helpeth alſo other griefs, as the pain in the Teeth and other hurts, if you have a ſtick wet in the Blood, and thruſt into the Oyntment, and there left. Alſo, if a Horſes foot be pricked with a nail by a Farrier or Smith, touch a ſtick with the blood, and thruſt it into the Box of Oyntment, and leave it there, it will Cure him. Theſe are the wonderful Gifts of God, given for the uſe and health of man.

CHAP. X.

The Weapon-Oyntment.

THere may alſo an Oyntment be made, where-with if the Weapons be anointed (where-with a wound is inflicted) the ſaid wounds ſhall be cured without pain. This is made as the other, except only ℥ i. of *Honey*, and ℨ i. of *Ox-fat* is to be added to this. But becauſe the Weapons cannot alwayes be had, the Wood aforeſaid is better.

CHAP. XI.

Against the Gout.

TAke of *Mummy, Maftick, Red Myrrhe, Olibanum, Ammoniacum, Oppopanax, Bdelium,* each ℥ ii. *Vitriol,* ℔ ii. *Honey,* ℔ ii. *Tartar,* ℥ i. ſs. *Aquavita,* gal. iii.

Let them be all Diftilled together into an Oyl. Then take little Flyes, ſuch as are bred in the dead Carcaſſes of Horſes, and make an Oyl of them, being well bruiſed. With which Oyl of the Horſe-flies, mix ℥ ii. with ℥ iv. of the other Oyl: Theſe two Oyls being well mixed together, let them be Diftilled again, and let this Diftilled Oyl be preſerved.

Then prepare the Characters, in manner following.

℞ of *pure Gold, pure Silver, filings of Iron,* each ℥ i. of *Lead,* ℥ ii.

Let them be all melted together in the hour of the *New Moon,* by a very ſtrong fire, that the filings of the Iron may be melted. For they will hardly melt, wherefore ſome *Boras* is to be added to them. Then let all the melted matter be
poured

poured out together upon a broad ſmooth ſtone,
that it may make a thin *Lamen:* for it cannot be
wrought with the Hammer afterwards, becauſe
of the Iron : afterwards, when ♄ is in Conjunction with ♂, in the ſame hour let the Characters,
Words, and Signes of the *Lamen* be engraven
thereupon, like two ſtamps of a piece of Money ;
and let them be finiſhed in that hour.

For the Gout.

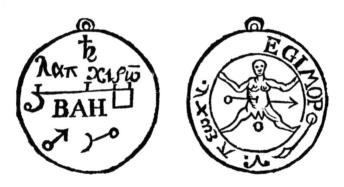

Let both the ſaid pieces of Money be engraven only on one ſide, in the hour of the ſaid conjunction of ♄ and ♂; and let them be ſo kept, that
they touch not one another.

Afterwards let there be made a *Sigil* of pure
Gold, not ſo thick as the other *Lamen :* when ♀ is
in Conjunction with ♄ or ♂, let the Characters,
Signes, and Words be engraven thereon. But
note , that the Seals are to be conjoyned together when there is a Conjunction of ♀ and
♄ : The ſecond face of the Golden Seal, marked

ed with the number 2, is to be turned against the engraven face of the superior Seal which hath not the Image of a man, and is marked with the number 4. But if ♀ be in Conjunction with ♂, then the second face of the Seal marked with the number 2, is to be turned upon the face of the upper Seal, which hath engraven upon it the image of a man, and is marked with the number 5. And when ☽ comes to the 6 degree of ♋ in the same order as is before shown, let the pieces of Money be both joyned together, the Gold being placed in the middle. Let them be all bored with one hole through the middle, and faſtened together with an Iron-wyer, and let the Patient hang them about his neck. And let his Members be anointed with the Oyl before preſcribed: hereby you ſhall try the powerful operations of Nature, even in ſuch as are 60 yeers old.

The Picture of Golden Money for the Gout.

A Sympa-

*A Sympathetical Oyntment againſt
the Gout.*

Let the Blood of the Patient afflicted with
the Gout, be reſerved : And that you may know
how to uſe it, Diſtil a Water from it in *Balneo
Maria.*

> Take hereof, ℥ vii. to which adde, of *Oyl of
> Roſes, Venice Sope,* each ℥ ſs. of *Man's
> Greaſe, Bears Greaſe, juyce of Sengreen,*
> each ℥ i. *Marrow of an Ox,* ℥ ſs.

Let them be all gently boyled in a veſſel of
Braſs, till they come to the thickneſs of an Oyntment ; continually ſtirring it, leſt it burn : Afterwards upon the eighth day of the *Moon's* encreaſing, let the Soles of the Feet of the Patient
be pricked with an inſtrument, as it uſes to be
done in Applications for the Winde : and the
place grieved being in this manner opened, let
them be anointed with this Oyntment very hot,
that it may penetrate. And by ſo doing 9 weeks,
he ſhall be Cured cleer of the Gout.

This Oyntment will laſt 10 yeers in its full
force and virtue, being kept in a cold place.

Chap.

CHAP. XII.

Against Contractures.

OYl of Sulphur against Contractures and shrinking of Sinews, is not to be contemned, but rather to be esteemed as a principal Remedy against such infirmities. This Oyl is made as followeth : Take of the best *Sulphur*, lb xv. Sublime it in a Cucurbite of Earth through a Glass Limbeck. Put the sublimed matter in a cool Cellar to disolve, and in success of time, it will be resolved into an Oyl. Then make the following Composition.

℞ of *Oyl of Sulphur*, ℥ ii. *Black Soap*, ℥ iii. *Aquavita*, ℥ v. *Oyl Olive*, *Oyl of Roses*, each, ℥ i.

Let all these be boyled, as the other, unto an Oyntment for the Gout ; always having a care that the flame take it not : Let the Members be very well anointed with this Unguent for 30 dayes ; causing the Patient to sweat in a dry Bath. It excellently helps contracted Members.

A Seal for Contractures.

Take what quantity you please of Gold thrice purified by Antimony ; or if you will, the weight
of

of a Ducat. Adde to it a little *Borax*, and melt it when ☽ is in the 19 or 20 degree of ♑; and caſt into it, as ſoon as it is molten, 30 grains of the filings of ♀ under the ſame hour. Which being melted and mixt together, pour them out together, and let them ſo remain until ☽ is in the ſame degree of ♏ : Then melt it again, and caſt in 30 grains of the filings of Iron, and pour it out again as at firſt. Then keep it till ☽ is in ♌ : and then form and faſhion it fit for the Sculpture; which ought to be done in the hour of ♃. You need not any further calculate according to the Courſe of ☽, till the Seal comes to be applied, having only reſpect to the hour beforehand, let the Signes which you ſee here drawn in the Figure, be engraven on both ſides of the Money: This Money muſt be ſewed up in a fine Cloth; and is to be hanged about the Neck by the Cloth only, and not by its own body, in the day and hour of ♃, ☽ encreaſing.

For **Contractures.**

CHAP. XIII.

For Womens Terms.

AN inordinate Flux of this Disease, doth extremely grieve many Women, sometimes divers years : by so much the more healthy and strong such women are, by how much they have their Courses in their ordinary seasons, and are then delivered from them. From whence arises a twofold way of reducing them into due order. The first is, to stay the Flux, and reduce it into a due course : the latter is to be used in the defects thereof, to provoke them to an ordinary Flux : the defect of them bringeth death ; wherefore to provoke them, let there be formed of pure Copper, without mixture of any other metal, a Seal in the hour of ♀, as is in the following Figure : But if the same cannot be perfectly finished in that hour, let it then remain unperfect until the same hour of ♀ comes again, and then perfect it : The form whereof must be this.

K

For

For the ᴍ*enſtrua.*

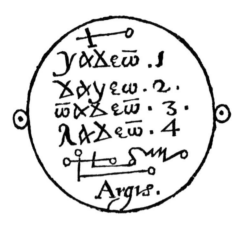

This Sigil ought to be formed with a File into one piece, and is to be bound with a ſtring upon the Back of the woman through two Rings, applying it at the beginning of the Back-bone upon the Teſtes, laying the Sculpture upon the fleſh, and that in the hour of ☽.

But if Nature ſuffer through too much abundant Fluxes, let the Characters be engraven in pure Silver in the hour of ☉, on both ſides of the Money, as they are drawn in the following Figure. Then let them be wrapped and ſewed up in ſilk, (for it muſt not be applied to the naked fleſh) and let it be bound upon the Navel of the Woman, turning that face next her body which is marked with the number 10. And afterwards when the Flux begins to ſtay, let her

wear

wear it 3 0 dayes, and then take it off: for if ſhe wear it any longer, there is danger leſt they be quite driven away and ſtopped ; and ſo cauſe a greater hurt than the firſt,

For the Menſtrua.

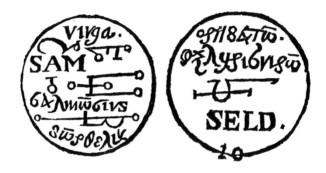

CHAP. XIV.

For the Leproſie.

THis Diſeaſe comes to the Lepers from their Nativity, and not only by accidents. Wherefore we have many other Remedies for them, conducing much unto the Cure thereof.   It is certain that *Aurum Potabile* drunk, doth palliate and hide the Leproſie, but not quite take it out of the blood.   The cauſe whereof is, becauſe every clean and ſound man hath Balſom, but the

K 2   Leprous

Leprous perfons have none in them; by reafon whereof alfo it comes to pafs, that they have no health in them: alfo, a congealed Member wanteth Balfom; and therefore it is infenfible when the ftrength of the Gold comes into the Stomack, which afterwards diftributeth it into the feveral Members of the Body; from thence refulteth a certain humidity which ingendereth the Balfom; wherefore the Leprofie ceafeth to increafe, fo long as there is any virtue or ftrength of the Gold in the Stomach. Alfo, a Phyfitian cannot know or difcern the Difeafe of Leprofie, if the Leprous perfon hath drunk Gold three dayes before his vifitation. We intend not to fpeak in this place of fuch as are manifeftly infected, but only of fuch whofe Difeafe is doubtful.

For the Leprofie.

If any do ufe the Sigil above written, and fuch like Remedies, let them not doubt of help. Let this kinde of Sigil be made of pure Gold, and wrought into a *Lamen* in the hour of ♄; but the Characters ought to be ingraven in the hour of ☉, when ☽ is in ♌,

and

and ☉ in the same sign ; which usually happens in *July*. Let it be hanged about the Leper in the hour of ♀, the Moon increasing : Let the Patient also drink Wine, wherein the same Sigil hath been some time steeped.

It ought to be renewed every year in *July*, for this Sigil loseth its force in a year.

The Leprosie working so strongly in the body of man, wherein it fixeth root.

CHAP. XV.

For the Vertigo.

MAny who do labour with this disease, the Heaven and Earth seems to them to turn like a wheel, and all things to run round. To others there seems a kinde of a Circle to flie before their eyes. This is a kinde of the Falling-Evil or Palsie more or less. For there is such a Convulsion of the Brain , that the Spirits of the Sight and the Brain, are impedited by a certain gross thick vapour ascending from the Stomach to the head, through the optick Nerves. Against this Disease make the Sigil which follows.

In the hour of *Mars*, and day of *Jupiter*, the *Moon* in *Aries*,which is the best Aspect of *Mars*; but see that she hath no evil Aspect from any other Planet.

K 3   The

Take of ☉ ℥ ſs. of ♂ ℥ ii. of ☽ ℈ v.

Let theſe 3 Metals be purely refined and melted together into one. Let them be poured out
and wrought into a very thin *Lamen*, and formed
with a little Ear ; afterwards when the *Moon* is
in the 12 degree of *Taurus*, engrave the Signes
which follow, and apply it to the Patient in the
hour of the *New Moon*, on the very point that
it firſt beginneth.

     Uſe this Remedy with the Seal :

     ℞ of *Organum, grains* 4.   Of *Unicorns-horn,*
       grains 2.   *Musk*, *grain* 1.   *Spirit of*
       Vitriol, grains 6.

Let them be adminiſtred every morning in a
ſpoon, about 3 a Clock after mid-night, continuing it 13 dayes ; and after every time taking it,
reſt one hour.

For the Vertigo.

CHAP. XVI.

For the Cramp.

MAke a mixture of *Sol, Luna, Venus,* and *Mars*; and let it be wrought into a *Lamen*, and thereof make a Sigil when the Sun is under the Earth, in the hour of *Saturne.* And then in the hour of *Jupiter* engrave these Characters and Signes with the words in the hour of the Sun; and apply it in the hour of the Sun when he is under the earth.

You may also make a Ring of the said Metals, on which engrave the same Signes, and wear the Ring on the finger of the Heart; but this ought to be done in the time, day, and hour before prescribed.

CHAP. XVII.

For the trembling of the Heart.

THe Hearts of men do sometimes suffer trembling, especially of Nobles and great men; for seldom doth this Disease take poor and mean men or women. From whence may be seen how God Almighty hath so artificially

K 4

distri-

diſtributed paſſions to every ſtate and Condition for their correction and admonition, without
reſpect of perſons. It is not to be numbered
amongſt eaſie Diſeaſes: for where it begins to
rule, it caſts the Patient upon the earth, and be-
reaveth him of ſtrength and ſenſe, and ſomtimes
of life. It riſeth from the Membranes and re-
ceptacles wherein the Heart is involved, it being compreſſed with corrupt and ill Flegm. A-
gainſt this, make a Sigil as follows, obſerving the
due times.

Firſt, in the day and hour of ☽, take of ☽ ℥ ſs.
which put and keep in a melting-pot until the
hour of the Sun, which is the 4 hour following
in the order of unequal hours; then melt it with
the fire, and the ☽ being melted, caſt in two
ounces of ☉ purely refined, as the ☽ ought to be:
theſe two Metals being well melted and mixt
together, leave them to cool in the Melting-pot
by themſelves, and keep them till the hour of
Venus next following: then melt them again, and
caſt in two drams of pure ♀, and pour it out; then
work it into a *Lamen* with a Hammer, & prepare
it ready for the engraving of the Signes: then
mark when the *Moon* and *Venus* behold one another with a good Aſpect; then engrave upon the
Money theſe two Signes which you ſee here.

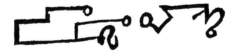

Afterwards

Afterwards in the point of the *New Moon* engrave thefe three Characters following under the other two.

Let it reft from that *New Moon* untill the next *Full Moon*, and in the point of that *Full Moon* in the fame face of the Money over all the Signes let thefe following words be written.

For the trembling of the Heart.

This being done, mark when the *Sun* enters *Leo*; and in the fame hour of his ingreffion, infcribe the Characters and Words you fee in the other figure, on the other-fide of the Money; and let them all be begun and ended the fame hour.

This Sigil being thus prepared and finifhed, is to be hanged about the Patients Neck in the
hour

hour and point of the *Full Moon,* that it may touch his naked fleſh upon his Heart.

Againſt this trembling of the Heart, there is alſo a moſt excellent ſecret ; our *Aurum Potabile,* and Quinteſſence of Pearl, of our deſcription, alſo oyl of Coral prepared as followeth.

The manner of Preparing Oyl of Coral againſt the trembling of the Heart.

℞ of *Coral,* ℔ i. Of *Common Salt, manip.* 3.

Let them be wrought into a moſt fine powder, and put it into a Glaſs ſtrongly Luted according to the ſequent deſcription: Take common Clay, or Potters white Clay, aſhes made of the bones of the heads of four-footed Beaſts, filings of Iron, Glaſs in powder, common Salt, Ceruſe, *&c.* which being wet, mingle them together, *&c.* put the luted Glaſs with the matter into Aſhes contained in an Iron Kettle, according to art ; kindle firſt a gentle fire, and increaſe it by degrees until the Spirit and Fumes do paſs into a Veſſel below ; then increaſe the fire more vehemently, until there remaineth no more moiſture. This Oyl is a moſt excellent Remedy for the trembling of the Heart, taken alone by it ſelf, without any thing elſe added to it.

An

An Appendix concerning Ruptures of
the Bones.

In what manner foever. Bones are broken, they are excellently well knit and confolidated, with the following Unguent, and are all orderly joyned.

℞ *Of Honey* ℥ ii. *Of Antimony, and Oyl of Vitriol* ℥ ii. *Of Badgers Greafe, Deers Sewet, Bears Greafe, and Sope, each* ℥ i. *Turpentine* ℥ i.ſs. *VVax* ℥ ii.

Let them be boyled into an Oyntment, and therewith let the Ruptures be anointed with a hot hand againſt the fire; it wonderfully Cures, Heals, and Confolidates, above all other.

The end of the firſt Treatiſe.

THE

The Second
TREATISE
OF
Celestial Medicines,

Containing,
The Mysteries of the Signes
Of the
Z O D I A C K.

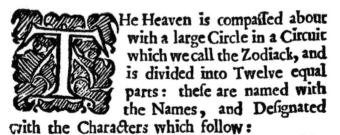

He Heaven is compassed about with a large Circle in a Circuit which we call the Zodiack, and is divided into Twelve equal parts: these are named with the Names, and Designated with the Characters which follow:

♈ *Aries*

♈ Aries.	♌ Leo.	♐ Sagittary.
♉ Taurus.	♍ Virgo.	♑ Capricorn.
♊ Gemini.	♎ Libra.	♒ Aquary.
♋ Cancer.	♏ Scorpio.	♓ Piſces.

The Seal of ♈ *is made of the following Metals.*

℞ ♂ ℥ ſs.   ☉ ʒ ii.   ☽ ʒ i.   ♀ ʒ ſs.

Theſe Metals, in the day, hour, and very point wherein the *Sun* enters the firſt degree of *Aries*, (which for the moſt part happens the tenth day of *March*, or thereabouts) are all to be melted together with a very ſtrong violent fire ; but firſt the Iron is to be reduced into filings, or elſe it will not be melted.   They being all melted and prepared, on the day of ♂, ☽ being in the 9 or 10 degree of *Aries* , or thereabouts, which is once every month : in the ſame hour it ought to be finiſhed ; but is to be applied when *Mars* is in the Ninth Houſe of Heaven, or the Eight.

Aries.

Aries.

This Seal is a moſt certain Experiment to Cure all Fluxes and Catharres deſcending from the Head upon the Brain, &c. For it purgeth the Brain, and drieth up all Flegm of the Head, and all Diſeaſes which appertain to the Head ; it amendeth all Maladies thereof, being worn night and day, the Signe of *Aries* being turned next the Brain.

The

The Seal of Taurus *is made of the Metals following.*

℞ Of ♀ ℥ i. Of ♃ ℨ i. Of ♂ ℥ ſs. Of ☉ ℥ ii.

They are all to be mixed together by melting them, the *Sun* being in *Taurus*, which every yeer happens about the eighth day of *April.* And in the very point of the *Suns* ingreſs into this ſigne, this Seal muſt be begun, and forthwith finiſhed, or elſe the whole work will be fru-ſtrate. And when the *Moon* is in the 1 o degree of *Taurus*, it is to be applied.

For the expedition of this work, there may be engraven ſome ſtamps of Iron firſt, wherewith the Seal may be coined after it is melted, where-by all the Signes and Words are quickly imprin-ted. So all the other Seals may be done: for oftentimes the hour ſlips away before they can be finiſhed, and then happens the greateſt detri-ment to this work. Wherefore the time is chiefly to be noted, as having the greateſt power in theſe operations.

Taurus.

Taurus

The Nature and Property of this Sigil, giveth a moſt excellent Remedy to them who have loſt their Generative Virtue : if it be ſo hanged that it may touch the Navel , the Sign *Taurus* being turned next the fleſh and the body, it giveth the beſt help to men or women.

The Seal of Gemini.

℞ of *Gold* and *Silver*, of each ℥ i,

Let them be both melted together the *Sun* entring the Signe *Gemini*; which happens about the 10 or 11 day of *May*, according to the courſe of the yeer. Wherefore the yeer wherein the

the Sigil is to be made, you muſt firſt calculate :
There are two *Lamens* to be made out of the
mixture of the aforeſaid Metals, whereupon the
Signes are to be engraven as they are poſited in
the following Figures, when the *Moon* is in the
ſigne of *Leo* or *Piſces* : but the Seal being per-
fected, is to be applied at ſuch time when ♀ is in
the firſt Houſe of Heaven ; the air gentle, milde,
and ſerene. That face of the Money that hath
the ſigne ♊, is to be turned towards, and worn
upon the naked skin : both the ſaid *Lamens* are
to be connexed together with a Circle made of
the ſame matter, almoſt a fingers breadth to be
aſunder in the middle, that they may not touch
one another, with theſe faces, or ſides, that are
without ſignes : for there muſt be ſo great diſtance between them, that there may be a Pipe
interpoſed, that may receive a Gooſe-quill full
of Quickſilver, and afterwards to be ſtopped
with Maſtick : it muſt alſo contain a Pipe of Metal, which muſt hold the Quill : when the work
is completed, let the Quick-ſilver be poured into the Quill, the day and hour of *Mercury*, the
Moon decreaſing.

The reſt was deſired in a German example,
even the ſtrength and virtue of this kind of Sigil,
for which it is made : but that we may not here
traduce you, until perhaps hereafter by ſome examples it may be made known ; we will not feign
any thing of our ſelves, which might agree therewith. In the mean time, if any have ſo great a
deſire to know the power and virtue thereof,
that they cannot ſtay in expectation of it, ſeek

to the moſt approved Authors in Aſtronomy, what are the Virtues of *Gemini*, in pro-
ducing Diſeaſes and other things: And then at
laſt, according to the proceſs of the preceding
and following Signes, maturely judge.

Gemini.

Cancer.

The Sigil of this Signe is made of moſt pure
Silver, in that hour when *Sol* enters the ſigne
Cancer, (which uſes to be about the 10 or 11
day of *June*) but when the *Moon* is in a good
Aſpect, and not afflicted by any evil Planet,
theſe Figures muſt be engraven in the hour of
the *Moon* when ſhe is increaſing: in the ſame
hour they muſt be begun, and finiſhed; or elſe
the whole labor is in vain.

Cancer.

Cancer.

This Seal muſt be applied in the day and hour of the *Moon,* ſhe decreaſing ; and is to be kept and worn very Clean. The Virtue thereof cau-ſeth happy Journeys: it is very profitable to be worn againſt the Dropſie, and all Defects of the Body proceeding from moiſture, or ſuperflu-ous Flegm.

Leo.

This Sigil of *Leo* is to be made with great di-ligence in *July* only, when the *Sun* is in his own Houſe, to wit, *Leo,* about the 13 or 14 day of the ſame Month. It is to be made of pure Gold, melted and wrought into a *Lamen,* when the *Sun* enters the firſt degree of the Signe, and per-fected before the end of the hour. Afterwards when *Jupiter* is in *Piſces,* the Signes are to be in-graven on one ſide thereof, as they are in the firſt Figure: And the other ſide is to be engra-ven when the *Moon* is in the Houſe of *Jupiter,* that is, in *Piſces.* And note, that after the mel-ting of the Seal, it muſt not be put again into the fire, elſe all things are in vain.

L 2

Leo.

Leo.

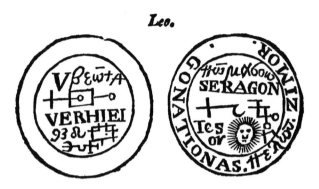

Let it be applied in the day and hour of the *Sun.* It hath a moſt excellent virtue : it cauſeth great Favours to men and women that wear it : It is a very good Remedy againſt Quartain Feavers. The Liquor is alſo good to be drunk, wherein it hath been infuſed all night. It is eſpecially approved againſt Peſtilence and all inward infection ; and againſt all Diſeaſes in the Eyes coming from heat, and from all other evil Heats and Rheums which we call flying Humors. It is good alſo againſt Burnings, the Seal being applied upon the place , certainly and ſurely draweth out the fire This way we cured the wife of one Mr. *Nicholas Barber* our Country-man, dwelling at a place called *Villach* in *Tranſylvania* ; who had a very great Burning, which we Cured, and drew out the burning ſo, that the burned place was healed without any ſore, or running Matter, only by applying ſuch a Sigil ; which ſhe wore upon the place until the end of the Cure.

Virgo.

Virgo.

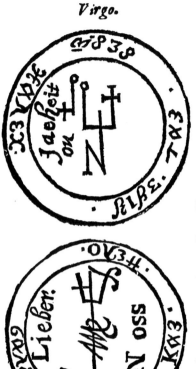

The Seal of *Virgo* is made of ♀ ℥ i. Of ☉ ℥ ſs. Of ☽ ℥ ii. ♃ ℥ ſs. Theſe Metals ought to be all melted together on Sunday about the 13 or 14 day of the *Sun*'s ingreſs into *Virgo*: And after they are melted, to be reduced into a thin *Lamen:* afterwards in the hour of *Mercury*, when *Mercury* is well Aſpected of the other Planets; let the Names and Characters be engraven upon the *Lamen*, ſo, that they may be finiſhed in the ſame hour.

Let it be applied when *Mercury* is in the firſt Houſe of Heaven, the air being clear and ſerene, (for then it is much better) and in the hour of *Mercury*, for then he ruleth the firſt Houſe of Heaven; but if it cannot be, refer it to an hour of like nature, although the hour of *Mercury* is beſt.　　　**L 3**　　　*Libra.*

Libra.

This Sigil is to be made of pure ♀, and to be melted, poured out and made when the *Sun* enters *Libra*, which ſomtimes happens on *Sunday* the 13 or 14 of *September*, according to the progreſs of the yeer: And this is to be noted, That when *Venus* is the ruling Planet, or Reſervator of the yeer, the Sigil will be of much more virtue, eſpecially if thoſe wear it, who were born under the ſame Planet; and if it be made and prepared for them. When ♀ is in the ſign *Libra*, the Signes, Charaƈters, and Words which you ſee in the following Figure, are to be engraven in the Seal; afterwards in the day and hour of *Venus*, in the firſt or eighth hour, which *Venus* governs, let it be applied.

Libra.

It is an admirable Remedy againſt all Bewitchings of Women, which hinder the aƈt of generation, and eſpecially in thoſe whom they hate: In brief, this Sigil is moſt profitable and excellent

excellent againſt all Maladies whatſoever ; eſpecially all griefs of the Secret Members.

Scorpio.

The Seal of *Scorpio* muſt be made of pure Iron
in the day and hour of *Mars,* when the *Sun* enters *Scorpio* , which happens about the 12, 13,
or 14 day of *October :* And in the ſame hour let
one ſide of the *Lamen* be engraven with his Characters. Afterwards, when the *Sun* is entered
into *Aries,* let the other ſide be engraven. It may
be applied at any time when you will.

Scorpio.

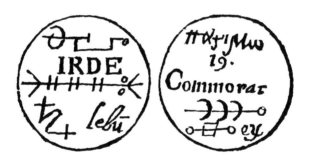

It is a moſt excellent Remedy againſt all Poy-
ſon and Diſeaſes thereby infected. It is excellent and admirable for Souldiers, Captains, and
ſuch as are in daily Controverſies : Alſo, if ſuch
an Animal as follows be made of pure Iron,
when *Mars* is Lord of the yeer, and the *Sun* enters the firſt degree of *Scorpio*; afterwards when

Mars

Mars is in his own Houſe in *Aries,* let it be engraven as follows. Then let it be applied in the
hour of *Mars :* the Houſe wherein it is hanged, it
defendeth ſafe from all Scorpions ; and all Serpents that are alive will flie out of it : it is a
moſt excellent Remedy againſt all venemous bi-
tings: mightily helpeth Souldiers in Fights :
and is very good againſt the Leproſie to be worn,
and the Patient to drink potable Gold.

Let it be engraven as this Figure.

Let there be affixed a Ring of pure Gold to
the Tayle thereof, that it may be worn hanging
about the Neck with the Head downwards. It
is a certain Remedy to drive away all Flies from
the Bed where it is hanged.

Sagittary.

This Sigil is to be made in the hour of the
Suns ingreſs into *Sagittary* (which annually happens on the 12 or 13 day of *November*) on the
firſt degree of the ingreſſion: let it be ſigned in
the hour of *Jupiter,* and applied in the ſame
hour,

hour, the *Moon* encreaſing. This is the ſecond Seal, that I knew after long ſearch and enquiry; and which, according to the Art that I profeſs, I have often uſed to the ſhame and ſcorn of my Adverſaries, that they have ſtood amazed like Aſſes, and durſt not open their mouths. There muſt be a ſilver Ring to hang it in, and it muſt be made of pure Tyrne, without addition of any other Metal; and to be wore and kept very clean : But it muſt be left off in the time of Copulation, or elſe it loſeth its virtue.

Sagittary.

We are again forced to complain of envious and perfidious men, who envying that in others, which they have not themſelvs, leave nothing perfect; that it may the ſecond time appear in this

Book, that their ſtrength and power is taken away, as above is done concerning the ſigne *Gemini;*

mini ; By the Proteſtation of the ſame Author, in this Chapter, when he ſaith, That this is
the ſecond Seal which he eſteemed to be moſt
powerful in the Medicinal Art, The envious
therefore labor in vain ; for whether they will or
no, he will bring into light every thing that they
have taken away out of the Books of *Theophraſtus Paracelſus.* For that Author before his death
did prudently incloſe thoſe Books in divers places in Walls ; ſo that if after his death, they were
loſt in one place, they might be preſerved in a-
nother, for good men; left that if any ſhould
come to the envious hands of wicked men,
ſhould be perpetually loſt, or torn in pieces.
Hereby they were preſerved for us whole, that
in due time the lives of wicked men, loving nothing but themſelves, may appear out of darkneſs.

Capricorn.

Now we come to treat of *Saturn* and his pro-
geny : this Seal is to be made of Gold ; for Lead
hath no operation with other Metals. There muſt
be

be made a Ring of Copper; and together with
the Seal, are both to be made in the hour when
the *Sun* enters *Capricorn*, and is fartheſt diſtant
from us; Let the Seal be engraven on the day
and hour of *Saturn*, and when *Saturn* is in a good
Aſpeƈt with ſome other Planet. It muſt be applied when the *Moon* is decreaſing or diminiſhed
in light: but the hour of the Aſpeƈt, whether it be
of the *Moon* or any other Planet, matters not,
This Seal may vulgarly be called the Sigil of Favor. This Seal throughly heals the Itch or Scurff
in the Thighes : Our Predeceſſors could not by
Art finde out the Cure of this Diſeaſe, accounting
it uncureable ; when as this is the beſt way to
Cure it, without any other means.

Aquary.

When the *Sun* enters *Aquary* in the Month
of *January*, let the Seal be made in the ſame hour,
of theſe Metals, being mixt and melted together :
of *Gold* ℥ ſs. *Lead* ℨ ii. of *Iron*. ℨ i. And when
the

the Planet *Saturn* is in the Ninth Houfe of Heaven, let thefe Signes and Words be quickly engraven one after another; you fhall not apply it till the *Sun* is under the Earth, and in the hour of *Saturn*; and then it is good, being hanged about the Neck, againft Contractures, cold Difeafes, and Sinewes fhrunk: it is very profitable to preferve the Memory, to get Favors amongft men, and very good againft all Poyfon, as may be proved by putting any venemous Spider upon the Sigil; it forthwith flieth away, and cannot poffibly remain upon it.

Pifces.

The Seal of *Pifces* is to be made in *February*, when the *Sun* enters *Pifces*, of the following Metals.

℞ of *Gold*, *Iron*, *Copper*, *Silver*, of each ℥ ii. Of *Tynne* ℥ fs.

Let them be all melted together, and the Seal formed

formed and engraven the fame hour of the *Suns* ingrefs ; afterwards let it be applied when *Ju-piter* is well placed in the eighth houfe of heaven, and in the day and hour of *Jupiter.* This is an admirable inftrument to loofe and expel Choler, of which do grow many grievous Difeafes, as Contractures, the Palfie, fhrinking of the Joynts, Burnings, *&c.* againft which it gives wonderful help to men or women : it mitigateth the pain of the Gout, takes away the Cramp, and all Griefs proceeding from Fluxes.

This Seal ought to hang down low upon the Navel.

Here

Here followes some more Com-
mon Secrets of Nature, of
Paracelsus.

Aving found a Conjunction of *Sa-*
turn and *Mars,* take a piece of
Iron, and frame a Mouse of it,
before the Conjunction passeth
over : and in the hour of *Jupiter,*
engrave upon the Belly of the
Mouse these words: ALBOMATATOX.
Afterwards, when the *Moon* is in the 9 or 10
degree of *Cancer* , on the right side engrave
ωπθεμῶ̃ερλιξ. Afterwards, the *Moon* descending,
and is in the 9 or 10 degree of the signe *Pisces,*
on the left side engrave as followeth : יורשתחב,
and upon the Back thereof, from the beginning
of the Back-bone unto the Tayle, engrave this
word, with the Character as you
see IO＋NATURA SUA.
Note that from the signe of *Ve-*
nus unto the Centre of the other
Character, a Line is to be drawn
over-thwart.   Then prepare a
Collary for this Mouse, of pure Lead, the *Moon*
increasing,

increasing, on the day of *Saturn*, and first hour of the night, which is the hour of *Saturn*; and engrave thereon these Characters, I L Con. 3. ♃. AB.E* λια*. This being thus performed, fit the Collary in the Conjunction of *Saturn* with *Mars* as abovesaid, and place it about the Centre or middle of the House, all kinds of Mice will flie away that are in the house: and if afterwards any Mouse come therein, he will not stay there an hour. And if any quick Mouse be bound with a thred to this Metallick Mouse, he will not live above an hour, but will die, and swell, as if he had eaten Poyson.

Of Sheep.

That we may not only have some means to drive away and expel hurtful Creatures, but also that we may preserve the profitable ; When Sheep are Corrupted with their Diseases, make a Sheep of Mudd as followeth:

Take Mudd, or Potters Clay, from three several places, much about the place where you live : Also, take Sand of a running Water about that place where for the most part Sheep drink; beat them all together when the Moon decreases : and of this Clay make the Image of a Sheep, under that hour wherein the Moon suffers her diminution: superscribe these following Signs with the Words here and there upon the Image.

EFERET.

. EFERET † HOGERET. †. JAGEREL. *ᴄᴠᴜῶᴛɪ*

Gᴀʌɪᴛɪ *ɣῶʋρῶʌ.* Sanor. Panor. Tanor.

Iʌῶʋϕ. Set this Sheep in the Sheep-fold ſprinkled over with Salt, and let the living Sheep lick it: And as many as lick it, or taſte of this Salt, ſhall not be infected, nor die with any Murrain or Rot of Sheep: And thoſe that are infected, by licking thereof, ſhall be Cured.

The ſame means may be prepared for Oxen, Kine, and Hogs; and other Animals; every one being prepared according to their natures, day, and time. Oxen and Kine have a Diſeaſe in their Blood, which cauſeth the Murrain in them; as Horſes ſomtimes ſuffer ſudden death through a Diſeaſe in the *Uvula.* For the Blood, write upon an Egg new laid,

Ambrammomis

Gorelis   Vortix

ᴏɪʌμῶ ῶαειχ   *ῶαμῶχ*

Open the Mouth of the Beaſt, and break the Egg upon his Tongue, and force him to ſwallow it, it, and it will forthwith heal it : but let him not drink in twelve hours afterwards.

The ſame is to be given to a Horſe : onely this excepted, that in ſtead of this Word and Sign, *Ambrammomis*, and the Croſs above, let there be writ this Word and Sign , *Kup-familon*, and then let him ſwallow it : afterwards give him a meaſure of Oats with Salt and Vineger, and afterwars he ſhall be cured in twelve hours : but preſently after he hath eaten the Oats , ride him an hour or two , that he may ſweat : then let him reſt. Theſe are the ſecrets of Nature, which are effected by times , dayes and hours; and without the obſervation of theſe, nothing can be effected.

Againſt Flyes.

Theſe Creatures do much infeſt men's houſes in Summer-time, and do corrupt and putrifie meat : to drive them away, do thus; make a Coffin of ſteel , and upon the Coffin engrave theſe Signs which you ſee in the Figure following.

And upon the Coffin , from the ſeparation of the ſaid Signs and Words, let there be engraven three lines tending towards the Cuſp: one in the new Moon, the ſecond in the full Moon, and the

third in the new Moon again. Afterwards, vnder
the Conjunction of ♄ and the ☽, write the words
and ſigns following.

If you fix this upon the Wall of an Houſe,
and draw a Circle round about it with Chalk, a-
bout the compaſs of a round Table, all Flyes
that are thereabouts will enter within the Circle, and there remain, until you take the Steel a-
way ; and then they will flie away, vexing men as
at firſt.

FINIS.

An Election of time to be observed in the tranſmutation of Metals.

IF at any time you ſhall deſire to tranſmute and change any Metal into another kinde, as Gold into Silver, or rather Silver into Gold, or any other Metal ; it is neceſſary, that you learn to elect a fit time for that purpoſe out of the Table following ; whereby you ſhall eaſily, ſooner, and without danger bring your Work to your deſired end.

A Table ſhewing the fit time when to tranſmute Metals.

To change into ☉.	☽ ♂ ♃ ♄ ☿	*Begin when the Moon is in the ſixth Degree of*	♋ ♉ ♈ ♓ ♒ ♍	*Alwayes begin in the hour of that Planet whoſe Metal you would change.*	☽ ♀ ♂ ♃ ♄ ☿
♄.	☉ ☽ ♂ ♀ ♃ ☿	*Twenty Degrees of*	♌ ♋ ♏ ♉ ♓ ♍		☉ ☽ ♂ ♀ ♃ ☿
☿.	☉ ☽ ♀ ♂ ♃ ♄	*Firſt Degree of*	♌ ♋ ♉ ♏ ♓ ♒		☉ ☽ ♀ ♂ ♃ ♄
☽.	☉ ♀ ♂ ♃ ♄ ☿	*In twelve Degrees of*	♌ ♎ ♏ ♐ ♒ ♊		☉ ♀ ♂ ♃ ♄ ☿

♀.

Reader, *thefe Books following are printed by* Nath.
Brooke, *and are to be fold at his fhop, at the* ʌn-
gel in Cornhil.

THat excellent piece of Phyfiognomy and
Chiromancy,Metopofcopie, the Symmetri-
cal Proportions and fignal Moles of the Body;
the fubject of Dreams : to which is added, The
Art of Memory. By *Ri. Sanders*. Fol.

Chiromancy : or , the Art of divining by the
Lines ingraven in the hand of Man by Dame
Nature; in 19 Genitures : with a learned Dif-
courfe of the Soul of the World. By *Geo.Wharton*
Efq.

Fons Lachrymarum : or, a Fountain of Tears,
with an Elegy upon Sir *Ch. Lucas*.By *J.Quarls*.8.

Hiftorical Relation of the firft planting of the
Englifh in *New England* in the yeer 1628. to the
yeer 1653. and all the material paffages happening there. Exactly performed.

That compleat piece called The exact Surveyor
of Land , fhewing how to plot all manner of
Grounds, and to reduce and divide the fame.
Alfo , Irifh Meafure reduced to Englifh Statute-
Meafure:ufeful for all that either fell or purchafe.
By *J. E.*

Milk for Children : or, a plain and eafie Method teaching to *Read* and to *Write* , with brief
Rules for School-Mafters to inftruct their Scholars in, and Mafters to inftruct their Families in.
By Dr. *Thomas.*

Culpepers Phyfical and Chyrurgical Remains, of
his own admired experience , never publifhed
before now by his Wife,being his laft Legacies.

Cul-

Culpepers Semiotica, or his Aftrological Judgement of Difeafes, much enlarged from the difcumbiture of the fick, which way to finde out the caufe, change, and end of the Difeafe. Alfo whether the fick be likely to live or die : with the figns of life and death by the body of the fick party, according to the Judgememt of *Hippocrates*. With a Treatife of Urines, by *N. Culp*.

Cornelius Agrippa his fourth Book of Occult Philofophy, of Geomancy. Magical Elements of *Peter de Abano*, the Nature of Spirits : made Englifh by *R. Turner*.

The Queens Clofet opened. Incomparable fecrets in Phyfick, Chyrurgery ; preferving, candying, and cooking, as they were prefented to the Queen, tranfcribed from the true Copies of her Majefties own Receipt-Books. By *W. M.* one of her late Servants.

The Conveyancers Light, or the Compleat Clerk & Scriveners Guide, being an exact draught of all Prefidents and Affurances now in ufe. By divers learned Judges, eminent Lawyers, and great Conveyancers, both antient and modern : whereunto is added a Concordance from K. *Rich.* 3. to this prefent.

A *Satyr* againft Hypocrites.

Wits Interpreter, the Englifh *Parnaffus*, or a fure Guide to thofe admirable Accomplifhments that compleat our Englifh Gentry in the moft acceptable qualifications of Difcourfe or Writing: Alfo, the whole Myftery of thofe pleafing Witchcrafts of Eloquence and Love are made eafie, in the Art of Reafoning, Theatre of Courtfhip, Labyrinth of Fancies, Love-Songs, Drollery ; The perfect Inditer of Letters, *A la mode*. By *J. C.*

FINIS.

♀.	☉ ☽ ♂ ♄ ♃ ☿	*Ninth Degree of*	♌ ♋ ♈ ♓ ♒ ♊	*In the Hour of*	☉ ☽ ♂ ♃ ♄ ☿
♂.	☉ ☾ ♀ ♃ ♄ ☿	*Eighteenth Degree of*	♌ ♋ ♉ ♐ ♑ ♍	*The Hour of*	☉ ☽ ♀ ♃ ♄ ☿
♃.	☉ ☽ ♀ ♂ ♄ ☿	*The third Degree of*	♌ ♋ ♎ ♏ ♒ ♍	*Hour of*	☉ ☽ ♀ ♂ ♄ ☿

Take this one Example only, and ſo work by the reſt : as, if you would change *Luna* into *Sol*, begin when the *Moon* is in ſix Degrees of *Cancer*, in the Hour of the *Moon*; and ſo obſerve of the reſt, according to this Table: for the obſervation of the time is not to be held of a vain account in the tranſmutation of Metals; for all negotiations and actions in this world are moſt happily brought to perfection, which are begun with due reſpect to the Courſe and influences of the Celeſtial Bodies; for our mor-

mortal Bodies are ruled according to the operations of the superiour Bodies of the Firmament, and they are ordained for that purpose by Almighty God the Creator; and do bring unto us, both health, sickness, infirmities, and health again : and in like manner the times are to be noted, and duly observed in Medicinal Operations, that their virtues may work the more powerful effects.

FINIS.